BUILDING QUALITY SERVICE

with competency-based human resource management

BUILDING QUALITY SERVICE

with competency-based human
resource management

Lynn van der Wagen

Disclaimer
This book is sold and distributed on the basis that neither the publisher nor the author are giving professional or technical advice and they disclaim any liability for the result of any action taken or omission to act by any person on the basis of the contents of this book. Readers are advised to seek independent legal advice in order to verify and evaluate information contained herein, in particular when writing letters of appointment and dismissal or using any of the forms etc. provided for discussion in the text.

Australia
  Butterworth–Heinemann, North Tower, 1–5 Railway Street, Chatswood, 2067
United Kingdom
  Butterworth–Heinemann Ltd, Oxford
USA
  Butterworth–Heinemann, Newton

National Library of Australia Cataloguing-in-Publication entry

---

van der Wagen, Lynn
  Building quality service.

  Bibliography.
  Includes index.
  ISBN 0 7506 8910 2

  1. Service industries–Australia–Personnel management.
  2. Personnel management–Australia. I. Title.

  658.300994

Illustration by Patrice Guilbert.
Cover designed by Zig Zag Productions.
Printed in Australia by Ligare Pty Ltd.

CONTENTS

PREFACE

The aim of this book is to integrate quality service concepts with those of human resource planning and development. Human resource planning is the process of determining the future staffing needs of the organisation. Sufficient staff with the appropriate skills, knowledge and other necessary attributes are needed to achieve the organisation's overall strategy. This strategy is affected by a number of external factors such as the economy, legislation (including industrial relations legislation) and changes in consumer behaviour. The aspect of the overall strategic plan that will be the focus for discussion in this book is the provision of service. Labour market trends have shown extraordinary growth in the services sector. To provide competent staff to meet the demands of the future, human resource managers and managers of small businesses need to address a number of aspects of human resource management as they impact on the service offered to customers.

These aspects range from job analysis, recruitment and selection to training and career development for staff working in service organisations. Such service organisations include Hospitality services, Communications, Health services, Maintenance, Utilities (waste management, fire, police, public services), Trading, Financial services, Professional services, Administration services, Technical services and Purchasing and Scientific services.

Quality system principles include the development of quality objectives, which should include:

- customer satisfaction consistent with professional standards and ethics;
- continuous improvement of the service;
- giving consideration to the requirements of society and the environment;
- efficiency in providing the service. (Australian Standards 3904.2–1992)

This book provides some clear guidelines for effective human resource management, the basis for any quality management program in the service industry. It takes a systematic approach to all issues, showing managers how to develop a learning culture that is responsive to changes, particularly changes in customer needs. In merging human resource management (including competency-based training) and quality management, the text provides clear guidelines for managers and trainers who want to keep both staff and customers for life.

After a theoretical start, this book becomes more entertaining and thought-provoking as it unfolds. Some readers might like to start with the last chapter, 'Ethics in service', and work their way back from there!

ACKNOWLEDGEMENTS

Writing this book would not be possible without the support of many people, only a few of whom are mentioned below:

- My husband and children for their unfailing patience while I sat at the keyboard surrounded by reference books.
- My students for their inspiration.
- My colleagues and the librarians at Northern Beaches TAFE, Brookvale for their assistance.
- Rosalie Karim and Gail McRae for their recommendation of myself for many, varied projects.
- Susan Briggs and Tourism Training Australia.
- Mark Day of the *Daily Telegraph Mirror* for the inclusion of his article.
- Standards Australia for the reproduction of their standards for Quality Service.
- McDonalds for the article on their Enterprise Competency Standards.
- The Sydney Renaissance Hotel, Thomas Cook, Victa and David Jones for giving permission to reproduce their advertisements.
- The *Sydney Morning Herald* (*SMH*) for their permission to reproduce their 'Column 8' snippets.
- Students of the Associate Diploma of Tourism and Hospitality at Northern Beaches TAFE, Brookvale for their research into customer expectations in the hospitality industry.
- The Educational Institute of the American Hotel and Motel Association for the use of their anecdote from their publication, *Ethics in Hospitality* (S. J. Hall, ed.).
- Pfeiffer and Company for permission to reproduce Gerard Egan's model for managing innovation and change.
- My Commissioning Editor, Helena Klijn, who ensured that this book was written and published in an extraordinarily short time.

1

QUALITY SERVICE DIMENSIONS

SUMMARY

This chapter builds a foundation for the rest of the book by highlighting service issues and defining service in terms of a model which is applied throughout the book. The difficulty inherent in incorporating highly complex and adaptable behaviours in definitions of service competence is previewed, with an overview of the remaining chapters which are based on key human resource management issues such as recruitment, selection and training of competent service personnel.

CHAPTER OBJECTIVES

On completion of this chapter you should be able to:

- define perception and explain its importance in customer service;
- identify reasons for perceptual differences;
- give examples of differences in perception relating to products;
- give examples of differences in perception relating to the procedural and personal dimensions of service;
- explain how you will train your staff to deal with customers' problems.

QUALITY SERVICE DIMENSIONS

This book is for managers and supervisors who want to employ and train staff to provide quality service. It integrates concepts in the fields of quality management and human resource management. The two go hand-in-hand, since it is the staff who provide the service, while the customers define whether the service meets or exceeds their expectations (see Figure 1.1). This interface between service personnel and customers is where complex communication processes occur, and it is this interaction at the front line of service delivery that is the focus for this book.

First, the concept of quality and the worldwide emergence of standards for quality service are discussed. Quality is defined in the customer's terms, and understanding the development of perceptions relating to products and services is one aspect of employee training in service provision. Recruitment, selection and training should be aimed at achieving positive customer perceptions of service.

Having addressed quality service from the viewpoint of the customer and looked at the international standards for quality service delivery, the second theme addressed is that of communication competence. What sorts of skills and knowledge are necessary to develop communication competence? Is this something one can learn? Is communication competence innate? Is it all a question of attitude—you either have it or you don't? Can employees who deal with customers on a daily basis use their experiences with customers as the basis for learning more about them? Can experiential learning help develop the culture we aim for, one in which employees cope intelligently with complex and changing circumstances, one in which employees communicate effectively with customers, both internal and external?

The third and final theme dealt with in this book is that of staffing and training in the service organisation. The enhancement of job descriptions to incorporate service and communication foci and the development of training methods that deal

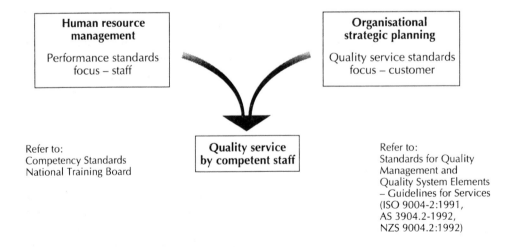

Figure 1.1   Performance standards for quality service

with non-routine as well as routine aspects of the job are all-important. Previous approaches have had a tendency to deal only with the routine tasks performed in a job, and yet it is agreed that each and every interaction with a client or customer is unique. Training methods need to address this aspect of employment in the services sector, to move away from simplistic formulae and to develop co-operative approaches that assist staff in understanding better the customers' needs and how to meet them in an appropriate way.

> **A COMPASSIONATE** effort from Government House. David de Carvalho, well-known city solicitor and cricketer, president of the Law Society in 1990–91, was awarded the AM for services to law and the community. He was to have been invested today, but, unhappily, fell gravely ill. On Monday night, the Governor, Rear-Admiral Peter Sinclair, and an aide, visited Mr de Carvalho at his Darling Point home. There, watched by the family, Mr de Carvalho received his honour from the Queen's representative. He died on Tuesday morning.
> (*SMH*, 22/9/94)

Organisations generally want to improve the standard of service they offer in order to increase competitiveness. In offering their staff training that assists in the achievement of improved service, an associated outcome is frequently an improvement in job satisfaction for employees and a corresponding reduction in labour costs. Standards for quality service, both local and international, are a useful guideline for improving the standard of service; note that the Australian and New Zealand Standards, AS 3904.2–1992 and NZS 9004.2:1992 respectively, are technically identical to the international standard, Quality Management and Quality System Elements (ISO 9004-2:1991).

The Australian Standard stresses several aspects of quality management in relation to staff and customers, as reproduced here in the appendix. These provide guidelines for the development of quality systems, and the remainder of this book demonstrates how a systematic approach to staffing and training can ensure that quality standards for service are met.

In most texts, quality management is referred to in terms of the quality of the product, this appearing to be a much easier thing to do than defining quality of service. Service is something quite intangible because it entails dealing with customers, with communication factors and most of all, with perceptions. Customers' perceptions of the quality of an organisation's products and services vary enormously, and so too do the employees' perceptions of the customers' perceptions. If this sounds complex, it is! Hopefully this book will go some way towards defining more clearly the communication aspects of customer service, and then using these as the basis for recruitment, selection, training and career development of service personnel.

PERCEPTION

Perception is the selection, categorisation and interpretation of stimuli. In plain English, this means that people all pay attention to different things and analyse them in different ways. In the service context, the uniforms worn by staff may be quite noticeable to some (but not all) customers. Informal personal presentation of staff may be quite noticeable to a customer from Europe or Asia, where formal dress is the norm for service personnel. However, informal dress is quite commonplace in Australia, where service staff in hot climates often work in colourful shirts and shorts. The fact that some customers immediately notice the dress code is not a bad thing. After noticing the informal attire, customers could then view this in terms of their own experience and upbringing. If formality is equated with professional service for the type of business concerned, the final evaluation may be that the dress is inappropriate and insulting. On the other hand, the sheer novelty of the colours and presentation, combined with other factors, may reinforce the image of a relaxed, friendly and informal culture. The reverse could also be true: where a department store or hotel is luxuriously decorated and the staff are dressed formally, the customers could themselves feel intimidated.

Customers have different perceptions which are influenced by their education, upbringing, experience and many other factors. To make life even more complicated, there are a number of other possibilities for perceptual differences:

- interpersonal perceptual differences—differences in views by different people;
- intercultural differences—differences in views by different cultures;
- intrapersonal differences—differences in views within the individual from day to day and moment to moment;

and also a multitude of yet other differences, based on age, income, interests and the like.

As service providers, reliant on customers' perceptions of our service, how are we to cope with this level of uncertainty? To answer this, we will look closely at the procedural and personal dimensions of service delivery.

In this book, the quality of products will not be dealt with in detail. Examples of products in the services sector are insurance policies, meals served in restaurants, hotel facilities, bank loans and holiday packages. As products are tangible and their quality more easily measured, we will deal instead with the more challenging aspect of quality service. This is the other dimension of service: the communication that occurs between the customer and the front-line staff who help to develop customer expectations and assist with the decision-making processes and problems. Communication has always been regarded as one of the most important skills required by staff.

In all organisations, people need to co-operate with others, and these interactions can be regarded as internal service provision. This internal service is provided to other individuals, departments and sections and is a key factor in quality management. Staff also communicate with external customers, on the floor, on the telephone and by fax or letter. In each and every one of these communications they develop expectations in customers, and help to meet them, frustrate them or exceed them.

Let us for the moment ponder some frustrated expectations. Booking a room at the Seaview Motel implies, does it not, that the motel will have a sea view? Isn't a major freeway that runs outside the front of the room is more likely to feature in the guest's perceptions than the glimpse of the ocean on the horizon?

In response to a complaint about an expensive swimsuit's colour running, 'We have examined the swimsuit and it is our opinion that there is definately [*sic*] no fabric fault. It would appear that the swimsuit has been rolled up damp causing the colour to run'. Well, what do you expect to do with a swimsuit?

'Yes, we'll send it right away,' as a response when ordering a meal for a hungry child, leaves the caller expecting that the meal will arrive promptly. A half-hour delay is enough to have parents on the verge of child abuse. If the service provider had given an estimate of twenty-five minutes or more, the parents could have changed the order or taken the child for a walk. Clearly there is a difference here regarding the words 'right away'. Frustrating the expectations of a guest, client or customer spells doom for any business. The customer's disappointment will be shared with other people and irreparably harm the organisation's reputation.

The case study below provides a transcript of an imaginary telephone conversation between a customer and a service provider, the travel agent. Notice the way the travel agent frustrates the customer immediately, and builds upon this by a series of mishandled misunderstandings. If you were the caller, would you recommend this travel agent to your friends?

CASE STUDY—WHERE IN THE WORLD IS BIRMINGHAM?

Wanting to book a flight, a customer dialled a travel agent listed in the *Yellow Pages*.

The telephone was answered at the twelfth ring.

TA: 'Moment please,' and the customer was kept waiting.

TA: 'Please hold,' until much later, 'Yes, how may I help you?'

C: 'I'd like to book a flight to Birmingham, please.'

TA: 'Your name is?'

The customer gave her name, which the agent typed into her computer, clearly with one finger searching for each key.

TA: 'That's "Pepedimitreou", is that right?'

C: 'No, it's P A P A D I M I T R I O U.'

TA: 'Right, Papadimitreou.'

C: 'No, D I M I T R I O U.'

TA: 'Oh right, I'll just start again. Could you spell it again, please? Your pronunciation is hard to understand.'

TA: 'Sorry, ma'am, I've got someone on the other phone, I'll just tell them to hold on, the other agent has gone to lunch and we're short-staffed to day.'

After a short delay, the travel agent asks, 'Are you right?'

C: 'What do you mean, "Am I right?"'

TA: 'Are you there?'

C: 'Yes, I'm here, where are you?'

TA: 'Sorry to keep you, ma'am. Can I have your address, please'
And after that, 'Your phone number?'
TA: 'How will you be paying for your ticket?'
All these issues finally resolved and entered into the computer using only one finger, the next question: 'And where did you say you wanted to go?'
C: 'Birmingham.'
TA: 'Can you spell that, please? Your accent is hard to understand.'
C: 'B I R M I N G H A M!'
TA: 'Which state is that in?'
C: 'It's not in a Australia. It's in England.'
TA: 'Sorry, I thought it was near Newcastle somewhere. I only do internal bookings. You'll have to call later to speak to James. He does the overseas flights. He'll be back in around an hour. See ya later.'
And with that the travel agent hung up.

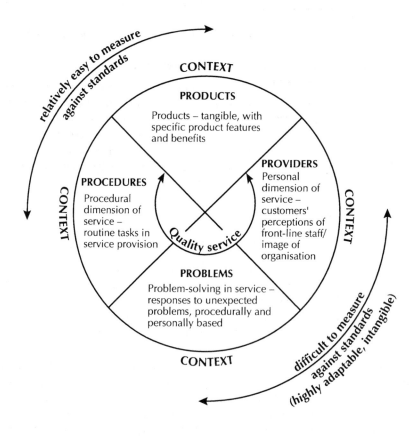

Figure 1.2 Model for quality service

Exceeding expectations is, however, the way to do business. A difficult thing to do, since in its marketing activities a company does the best it can to communicate the fine features of the organisation's products and services. By doing this to build up expectations, it makes it all the more difficult for the organisation to exceed them. In most cases, expectations are constructed by advertising product features and benefits. Added value then occurs when a staff member develops a rapport with the customer, offers extra assistance, information or advice. In some cases, a friendly conversation is a real bonus for a lonely customer (but for others it is an intrusion on their privacy). A flexible approach when dealing with a wide range of people and an ability to perceive and adapt to their needs is one of the staff attributes we will be looking at later in the book. It is an example of a possible way to exceed a customer's expectation.

The delivery of total quality service is thus highly dependant on the customer's perceptions of the organisation, its products, its procedures and the way it deals with complaints and problems. The model for quality service is given in Figure 1.2. In the model, service is described in terms of three dimensions. These are useful in that they provide a focus for recruitment and training, and these dimensions will be described in detail in this and subsequent chapters.

An evaluation of poor service is often attributable to four factors, as follows.

Differences in perception relating to product

Differences in perception occur between the product the organisation provides and the customer's expectations of that product. Products are tangible. They are things that can be touched and felt, eaten or worn. Products include food items, garments, electrical goods, motel beds and the like. Other products are specified on paper, such as insurance policies, bank accounts and holiday packages. In each case the quality of the product can be evaluated or judged relatively easily, certainly in comparison with the following aspects of service delivery. For this reason, therefore, this book is not going to deal with customers' perceptions of product quality in any detail.

Differences in perception relating to procedure

Differences in perception occur between the procedures the organisation follows and the customers' expectations of those procedures. Many of these procedures are routine, standardised operational methods defined by the organisation. In most cases both staff and customers are quite used to these procedures. In a restaurant you expect to be shown the menu and left with it for a short time while you decide what to order. There is a fairly standard time at which you, the customer, would start to look around wondering why the waiter had not returned. The time span for this procedure is quite short. The customer would expect a longer delay while the meal is prepared. All these procedures are fairly similar from one restaurant to another, and the waiting periods comparable. However, the procedure could be quite different in an establishment where you are expected to help yourself to a plate, select what you want from an overhead menu, tell the chef behind the counter what you would like, watch the preparation of the meal, and then pay the cashier. This can be quite daunting to a customer who has never experienced this type of service before.

In supermarkets procedures include things like taking a numbered ticket for service at the delicatessen counter. It is most annoying to find out about the procedure when you have been waiting for service for some time, blissfully unaware of their methods. Stores, in accepting credit cards, require authorisation once a limit is exceeded. This is a routine procedure, with most customers understanding the need for a telephone call to check with the credit card company. Training staff to follow such procedures is straightforward, since the steps involved are standard. Competency-based training, in the development of skills for the performance of routine tasks is well underway in most industries. Once standard operational procedures are defined, a task analysis will enable the trainer to plan training and assess competence. Further examples of skills relating to routine procedures include the exchange of traveller's cheques, balancing the till at the end of a day's trading and opening and stocking an area in preparation for trading. Most courses that train the trainer give supervisors the skills to train staff to follow routine procedures. This is only half of what service entails. The second and arguably most important training for competent staff in service industries is training in the personal aspects of service, described in the next section.

Differences in perception relating to provider (personal dimension of service)

Differences in perception occur in the way customers are treated and the way they expect to be treated. This aspect of service is the most challenging, particularly when it comes to competency-based training, which needs to assess non-routine, adaptive responses to customers and their needs. Depending on the circumstances surrounding the interaction with the customer, such as pressure resulting from customers waiting, the service provider is expected to display some (if not all) of the following skills:

Greet the customer appropriately
Use body language cues to estimate whether the customer is in a hurry
Use questions to fully establish customer needs
Use non-verbal cues to establish customer needs
Listen attentively
Time interventions appropriately
Remember the customer's name and previous details
Offer products in a positive light
Tailor language to meet the customer's needs
Use a positive tone of voice
Demonstrate confidence through volume of speaking
Modify body language and use appropriately
Present self as an ambassador of the organisation
Adapt level of formality to suit the situation

Assist the customer in reaching a decision
Close the sale
Thank the customer even if sale is not concluded
Follow up on customer's unmet needs
Seek feedback on products and procedures.

All of the above may result, for example, in the assessment that the customer is in a hurry, knows exactly what he wants and that the provider is unable to meet this need. In this case, the communication may be very brief indeed, concluding with a simple apology. In another situation, in which the customer is a regular, there may be a conversation about unrelated topics (such as family or weather), discussions relating to a range of products and a lengthy decision-making process before the sale is concluded. The customer may wish to go away and think about the decision and the staff member then needs to follow this up further.

The contrast between these two types of communication with customers illustrates the level of adaptability required for successful customer relations. Each and every one of these 'moments of truth', as they have been termed by the former Scandinavian Airlines president, Jan Carlzon, is unique. And the resulting perception of the service provider is critical to the success of any organisation. The term 'service provider' is used deliberately. At the front-line, perception of service is usually based on the interaction the customer has with a staff member. It must be stressed, though, that the resulting perception covers more than that relating to the individual with whom the customer was dealing; it covers that also of the business or organisation as a whole. The front-line service personnel represent the organisation to the customer, so the resulting perception is of the *organisation* as a service provider. The actions of staff are identified with the organisation's image. A telephone company, retail outlet, bank, restaurant or hotel develops an image in the minds of their customers, based on their interactions with staff.

Differences in perception relating to problem-solving

It could be argued that problem-solving or complaint handling belongs in the previous section. However, since this forms such an important part of the customer's perception of the quality service the organisation offers, it will be dealt with separately. As in the previous discussion, problem-solving involves one-off, unique and, hopefully, unexpected requests for assistance and complaints. The ability of your staff to deal with unique, unusual and problematic situations is crucial to the success of your operation. Can one really train staff to deal effectively with all problems? How can they provide quality service in a competent

ON A VISIT to the city, Jill Hayes, of St Albans, bought a postcard for a friend, Eva Clarke, of Vaucluse, wrote a message on it, and dropped it in a letter receiver at Double Bay. Not until she was driving home did she realise she hadn't put a name and address on it. She rang Australia Post, speaking to "David" and "Les" at the sorting branch at Alexandria. Could they help? She left a description of the postcard, and the intended address. It arrived in a couple of days in an Australia Post envelope. They're legends.
(SMH, 8/10/94)

manner? How do we know whether the problem was successfully resolved? If it was, was it successful from the customer's point of view or from the company's point of view? If we don't know how to anticipate the situation that will occur, how do we prepare staff to deal with it? There are three key ways in which these issues can be tackled:

- give your staff the knowledge they need to apply to creative solutions;
- give your staff the skills they need to apply to these situations;
- create a learning cycle in which complex situations are carefully analysed so that they provide a solid experiential base for future situations.

An acknowledgment of the validity of customer perceptions and a willingness to seek feedback and act on it are key aspects of quality service management. An understanding of perceptual factors, decision-making, attitude formation and the like should enable staff to provide more satisfactory service on a personal level. Some experience in utilising skills, such as listening and questioning, will further improve their range of methods for communicating with customers. Finally, trainers and managers need to develop in their staff the ability to learn from experience, to analyse, to instantly choose effective responses, to apply them appropriately, to monitor success in the eyes of the customer and to evaluate holistically.

MANAGING HUMAN RESOURCES FOR THE DEVELOPMENT OF SERVICE COMPETENCE

A good analogy for the personal and procedural dimensions of service is the scoring of ice-skaters in figures competition. The first score is for technical merit. This relates to set minimum standards for defined manoeuvres, such as jumps and spins. In the service industry, procedures define the routine performance of tasks such as processing payments, and there are naturally corresponding standards. The other score allocated to the ice-skater is for artistic merit. This is the artistic interpretation, the choreography and grace of the movements to match the mood of the music. Judgements of artistic merit are more subjective but, generally speaking, consistency is achieved by professional judges. In service, customers are superb professional judges of the artistic interpretation of service delivery. For them, the personal dimension of service is just as important as the routine procedural dimension which they take for granted unless something goes wrong.

Having discussed service and having teased out what we mean by the term 'quality service', we can now base our management of human resources in the organisation on sound service principles. If we carefully define our expectations in terms of communication skills required for our employees, we will be able to recruit more suitable candidates, select the best person for the job, and train staff to meet these requirements for superior service delivery. The first chapters in this book therefore deal with service in some detail. In later chapters we turn to human resource management issues of recruitment, selection, training and career development of staff in the services sector.

QUALITY SERVICE MANAGEMENT

Using competency standards as the basis for selection, for training and for career development, managers are able to design systems that allow their employees formal recognition for their achievements where their industries have developed competency standards recognised by National Training Boards. These standards have already been developed in Australia for a wide range of industries including retail, insurance, hospitality, community services, police, small business and telecommunications. In many cases, these competency standards form the basis for industrial relations awards and agreements, thus ensuring that career progression, based on competency-based training and assessment, is linked to remuneration. Industry-developed competencies thus form the basis for performance measurement. These competencies and associated standards are dynamic and responsive to changes in the business environment. In this way, individual employee performance is linked to organisational goal setting and strategic planning. Standards that fully reflect all dimensions of quality service are the blueprint for success for both individuals and their employers.

EXERCISES AND DISCUSSION

1. How would you define perception?

2. Consumer decision-making is influenced by a range of factors. Can you think of a recent purchase (new policy, holiday, meal, computer) and list some of the factors that contributed to the decision you reached. Why were competitors unsuccessful in getting your business?

3. Explain your worst experience as a customer. Decide whether the problem was with the product, the procedural or personal dimension of service, or an inability on the part of the provider to solve your problem? Or it was a combination of all three?

4. Review the case study on pages 5 and 6. Describe the performance of the travel agent. Use this description to give some advice on ways in which customer service could be improved in such situations.

5. Times have changed more than we realise. This customer has shared a few perceptions with us. Do you think in each case that the product has changed, the procedure or the personal dimension of service?

    Those were the days when ...

        customers were 'sir' or 'madam'.
        only girls wore earrings in their ear lobes.
        staff were not encouraged to fraternise with the guests.
        cash was an acceptable method of payment.

harassment wasn't taken seriously.
you were issued with a simple key to get into your room.
you could open the windows.
the doorman could be identified by his top hat.
you had to call room service to get a strong drink.
bushwalking was the last thing you would do on a holiday.
people smoked in restaurants.
children had dinner at home.
eating out meant you were served.
you went on a cruise to relax.
nightclubs opened before midnight.
drinks were poured with a free hand.
'welcome back' meant that they really remembered you.

APPENDIX

Quality Management and Quality System Elements, Part 2: Guidelines for Services

Reproduced from Australian Standards 3904.2–1992 (NZS 9004.2:1992 / ISO 9004-2:1991), pp. 8, 9.

5.3   PERSONNEL AND MATERIAL RESOURCES

5.3.1   General

Management should provide sufficient and appropriate resources to implement the quality system and achieve the quality objectives.

5.3.2   Personnel

5.3.2.1   Motivation

A most important resource in any organization is that of the individual members of personnel involved. This is especially important in a service organization where the behaviour and performance of individuals directly impacts on the quality of service.

As a spur to the motivation, development, communication and performance of personnel, management should:

- select personnel on the basis of capability to satisfy defined job specifications;
- provide a work environment that fosters excellence and a secure work relationship;
- realize the potential of every member of the organization by consistent, creative work methods and opportunities for greater involvement;
- ensure that the tasks to be performed and the objectives to be achieved are understood, including how they affect quality;
- see that all personnel feel that they have an involvement and influence on the quality of service provided to customers;

- encourage contributions which enhance quality by giving due recognition and reward for achievement;
- periodically assess the factors which motivate personnel to provide quality of service;
- implement career planning and development of personnel;
- establish planned actions for updating the skills of personnel.

5.3.2.2 Training and development

Education brings awareness of the need for change and provides the means whereby change and development can be accomplished.
Important elements in the development of personnel include:

- training executives in quality management, including quality-related costs and evaluation of the effectiveness of the quality system;
- training of personnel (this should not be restricted to those solely concerned with quality responsibilities);
- education of personnel on the service organization's quality policy, objectives and concepts of customer satisfaction;
- a quality-awareness programme which may include instruction and training courses for new entrants, and periodic refresher programmes for longer-serving personnel;
- procedures for specifying and verifying that personnel have received suitable training;
- training in process control, data collection and analysis, problem identification and analysis, corrective action and improvement, team working and communication methods;
- the need to assess carefully the personnel requirements for formal qualifications and give appropriate assistance and encouragement where necessary;
- the performance evaluation of personnel to assess their development needs and potential.

5.3.2.3 Communication

Service personnel, especially those directly involved with the customer, should have adequate knowledge and the necessary skills in communication. They should be capable of forming a natural work team able to interact appropriately with external organizations and representatives to provide a timely and smooth running service.

Team activities, such as quality improvement forums, can be effective for improving communication between personnel and can provide an opportunity for supportive participation and co-operation in solving problems.

Regular communication within the service organization should be a feature at all levels of management. The existence of an appropriate information system is an essential tool for communication and for service operations. The methods of communication may include:

- management briefings;
- information exchange meetings;
- documented information;
- information technology facilities.

2

QUALITY SERVICE MANAGEMENT

SUMMARY

In this chapter, the model of service introduced in chapter one will be discussed further with illustrations. This discussion applies to the services sector in general, giving examples for retail sales, hospitality, banking and the like. An attempt will be made to clarify quality service issues and what is meant by 'competence'. Finally, both topics will be merged to form human resource management and development policies that will ensure continuous quality improvements in service, and ongoing learning and career development for personnel.

CHAPTER OBJECTIVES

On completion of this chapter you should be able to:

- discuss what is meant by quality service;
- explain competency-based training and describe the value it has in meeting service standards;
- explain why it is inappropriate to be too detailed or specific when describing service performance;
- discuss whether you think giving quality service is an art or a science;
- develop a model for service competence using a two-way table of tasks and attributes.

QUALITY SERVICE MANAGEMENT

Essentially, the delivery of quality service entails the development of and adherence to policies and procedures. Generally speaking, this is the foundation for quality management in manufacturing industries and the basis for measurement of quality. However, another key factor in the delivery of quality service is the development of customer expectations relating to the products and services, and the ultimate decision on the part of the customer as to whether these expectations were met or exceeded. Given that individual perceptions vary enormously, one important aspect of service delivery is tuning into customer needs, understanding their perceptions and delivering service accordingly. This highly adaptive communication process, which forms the basis for the personal dimension of service, cannot be simply defined in terms of the type of standards that were more easily applied in the area of procedures. Nonetheless, by acknowledging the complex nature of the interaction with the customer and the flexibility required for the delivery of quality service, one can go a long way towards selecting and training staff who can not only follow company procedures, but can also respond appropriately in developing customer expectations and meeting or exceeding them. The perceptions of both the customers and the service personnel are core communication concepts, and will be acknowledged and discussed further in the next chapter.

MRS CONNIE Wright, of Kurraba Point, got a call one night recently from a John Gill, of State Transit, to say her purse had been found. It was only then that she realised she'd lost it—on the 5.50 pm ferry to Neutral Bay. Now that's quick service.

(SMH, 14/7/94)

One of the most controversial discussion points in the development of competency standards is the issue of dealing with the unexpected (in the model of service introduced in chapter one, this is referred to as problem-solving). Unexpected situations form the basis for much of our work in the services sector. In solving problems we need to adhere to procedural and policy guidelines, while acknowledging the customer's unique perceptions, needs and expectations for positive outcomes.

SERVICE AND COMPETENCE

In the most simplistic sense, quality service is service which is 'good' in the eyes of the customer.

Competent service should be 'good service', as defined by customers. It is not always defined that way by management. Too often staff are given reasons for procedures such as 'We do it this way because it saves time' or 'We do it this way because it reduces costs', rather than 'We do it this way because our customers like it this way'. Managers therefore have numerous criteria by which they judge the performance of their staff, and the aim of this book is to raise their consciousness of the most important outcome: pleasing the customer.

Competent service is the application, by employees, of appropriate skills and knowledge to the performance of a task, the ultimate aim of which is customer satisfaction. Staff training is too often focused on the needs of the organisation, instead of on the needs of its customers. Training in service industries should be aimed at developing competent staff, whose skills and knowledge are brought to bear on the perennial dilemma, how best to meet the customer's needs.

The merging of the customer perception of 'quality service' and the management perception of what 'competent service' looks like occurs when quality management meets competency-based training in the definition:

> QUALITY SERVICE IS SERVICE, DELIVERED BY COMPETENT PERSONNEL,
> WHICH MEETS OR EXCEEDS CUSTOMER EXPECTATIONS.

Other theorists prefer to define 'quality' as meeting a standard. If those standards are set in response to customer needs, then the definition suggested here is acceptable: its aim is to stress the role of the customer in evaluation of service.

The objective of this book is to utilise current thinking in the fields of competency-based training and quality management. In order to do this, some discussion relating to competence, with definitions and corresponding assessment techniques, is a useful starting point. Following this, further discussion relating to quality management, with a merging of both ideas, is the basis of this chapter.

COMPETENCY-BASED TRAINING AND DEVELOPMENT

'Competency' is the current buzz word in the services sector. Is it, as some writers hope, another passing phase? Australia is not alone in its interest in competency-based training. Our movement towards competency-based training and recognition of prior learning is mirrored in Europe and America. The reasons for the emergence of competency as the panacea for training and career development provide some clues as to the permanency of the concept at the core of future developments in education.

Developments in transportation and communication have led to greater flexibility in the global work force, with more frequent movement resulting from international trade and increasing interdependence. Individuals moving from firm to firm, state to state and country to country are demanding that their professional skills are recognised. Thus, the goals of the competency movement are national and international certification.

Industry is also looking for better information regarding educational outcomes and the value these have in employment. Superficially, it would appear that economies can only benefit from an increased emphasis on defining industry needs, but this approach has potentially serious limitations if these goals are short-sighted and narrowly defined. Efforts to define elements of competence in unambiguous and specific terms also have the potential to lead to 'a never ending spiral of specification' (Wolf 1993). In Australia, however, the emerging model of competence (Hager, Athanasou & Gonczi 1994) is more holistic, integrated and judgemental: 'This richer conception of competency views competencies as attributes of workers that underpin competent performance of an occupation'.

In the delivery of customer service the staff are required not only to skilfully integrate and manage a range of discrete tasks, but also to modify these procedural service aspects to meet customer needs. In addition, the personal dimension of service demands the integration of social skills in the development of customer relationships. It has been suggested that loneliness brought about by the fragmentation of families (among other factors) has led to the need of customers to be recognised as individuals. This implies developing a deeper relationship in a shorter space of time than was ever the case in service provision in the past. Intimacy, in a slightly superficial sense, is created more rapidly than ever before. Hence the increasing focus on social dimensions of service in the hospitality, tourism, banking, insurance, fitness and recreation sectors.

Hugh Mackay, in his research into the mind and mood of Australia in the 1990s, suggests that holidays have an enormous emotional significance for many Australians who seek predictability in their escape from the chaos of daily existence and are 'seeking a cocoon of perfection' (1993, p. 222) in which relationships with family and community can be more satisfactory.

Returning, however, to the competency movement, a definition of competency on which much work in Australia has been based is as follows:

> *Competency* comprises the specification of knowledge and skill and the application of that knowledge and skill to the standard of performance required in employment. The concept of competency includes all aspects of work performance. This includes:
>
> • performance at an acceptable level of skill
> • organising one's tasks
> • responding and reacting appropriately when things go wrong
> • fulfilling a role in the scheme of things at work; and
> • transfer of skills and knowledge to new situations.
>
> (Hager, Athanasou & Gonczi 1994, p. 10)

Assessment of competence involves collecting evidence and making judgements on whether competency has been achieved. It needs to be ensured that this evidence is wide-ranging and a valid reflection of the individual's skills and knowledge. Assessments also need to be reliable over a period of time. Hager, Athanasou and Gonczi (1994, p. 7) provide a continuum of competency-based assessment that is most useful, reflecting the range of assessments which can take place. This continuum is reproduced in Figure 2.1. At the end of the scale, where there is direct assessment of workplace performance, underpinning knowledge and particular skills are 'holistically subsumed' into this performance.

Certainly, the wider the range of assessments, the more valid the assessment of competence. Educators will argue, however, that competence requires more than workplace assessment, since many aspects of knowledge and their application are never (or are rarely) tested in everyday situations. For an employer, it would be

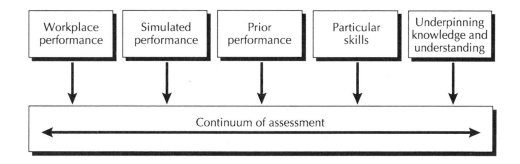

Figure 2.1 Competency–based assessment continuum
(Source: *Assessment Technical Manual,* Paul Hager, James Athanasou & Andrew Gonczi,
AGPS, Canberra, 1994, p.7. Commonwealth of Australia copyright reproduced by permission.)

desirable that employees know about risks to health and safety, such as transmittal
of infections such as hepatitis, or about anti-discrimination, trade practices
legislation and the like, without these being tested in practice. Errors, where they
occur could incur liability which would be tested in court—rare occurrences one
hopes, but requiring a substantial knowledge of risk and liability on the part of
employees.

Recognition of prior learning

Increased recognition of informal learning as the means by which many an
individual reaches a high level of expertise without formal education has led to
demands that assessment occur in the workplace granting recognition for these
skills. In Australia the movement has gained momentum across a wide range of
industries. The Commonwealth State Training Advisory Committee (COSTAC)
Working Party provided a definition of competency-based training in 1990 that
has relevance in the recognition and certification of informally acquired skills and
knowledge:

> Competency-Based Training is concerned with the attainment and
> demonstration of specified skills, knowledge and application to minimum
> industry specified standards rather than with an individual's achievement
> relative to that of others in a group. It is criterion referenced rather than
> norm referenced. (COSTAC 1990, p. 33)

Utilising industry-defined standards, recognition of prior learning is underway
in a number of industries. This enables individuals to complete assessments of
modules or units of competency, and to receive formal recognition for having done
so. In the hospitality industry, for example, employees who do workplace
assessments conducted by licensed assessors are given certification for having done
so. Since these same modules form the basis for curriculum design in colleges and
universities, this entitles the person to exemptions in subjects or areas that have

already been assessed. Use of industry-designed competencies as the basis for national curriculum development also ensures portability of qualifications from state to state.

Model for assessment and appraisal

The model for assessment discussed in this chapter is a useful one, and will be further developed and utilised in later chapters. This two-dimensional integrated approach, suggested by Gonczi, Hager and Oliver (1990), lists tasks on one axis and the knowledge, abilities and skills required to perform those tasks on the other axis (see Figure 2.2).

Burg, Lloyd and Templeton (1982) suggest that a third dimension could be added to develop a matrix for the medical field. The key tasks performed by general practitioners form one axis, and the attributes that are required to perform these tasks form another (knowledge, problem-solving, attitudes, interpersonal skills and technical skills). The third dimension represents different areas of practice in which competence would need to be demonstrated (such as with pregnant and elderly patients).

In the first chapter the following staff attributes were suggested and could form one axis.

> The service staff should be able to:
> use body language cues to anticipate customer needs
> use questions to fully establish customer needs
> use non-verbal cues to establish customer needs
> listen attentively
> time interventions appropriately
> remember the customer's name and previous details
> offer products in a positive light
> tailor language to meet the customer's needs
> use a positive tone of voice
> demonstrate confidence through volume of speaking
> modify body language and use appropriately
> present self as an ambassador of the organisation
> adapt level of formality to suit the situation.

> The second axis would be formed by the service staff's performance of the following tasks:

> greeting the customer
> offering assistance
> describing the product's features and benefits
> assisting the customer with decision-making
> processing the payment
> thanking the customer.

The first list describes what the employee should be able to do; these skills can be brought to bear where appropriate. The second list describes the tasks involved or

Tasks (procedure)

Provider skills	Greeting the customer	Offering assistance	Describing product features and benefits	Assisting customer with decision-making	Processing the payment	Thanking the customer
Use questions to fully establish customer needs						
Use non-verbal cues to establish customer needs						
Listen attentively						
Time interventions appropriately						
Remember customer's name and previous details						
Offer products in a positive light						
Tailor language to meet the customer's needs						
Use a positive tone of voice						
Demonstrate confidence through volume of speaking						
Modify body language and use appropriately						
Present self as an ambassador of the organisation						
Adapt level of formality to suit the situation						

Figure 2.2   Procedure and skills for service

the procedure involved in making a sale. The two lists are displayed in Figure 2.2. Notice that frequently the performance of a task requires the application of more than one attribute.

Procedure and skills for service

Following the previous discussion, a further dimension could be added: context. The importance of the client, and their long-term value to the organisation or business, is a consideration when deciding how much time to spend with them. Other contextual factors are shown in the three-dimensional matrix for service delivery, Figure 2.3. Service is thus varied depending on the potential value of the customer to the business, the time available for service and the type of customer (these are many and varied, referred to by marketers by the impersonal term 'market segments'). For example, the potential damage to the business' reputation by the media would ensure that the service provided a journalist would be of the highest standard, the risk factor in this situation being very high. A regular customer kept waiting would be the lesser risk when staff are under pressure. Excessive demands by customers coupled with understaffing is frequently the context in which staff are expected to perform competently and it would be unrealistic for us to suggest otherwise.

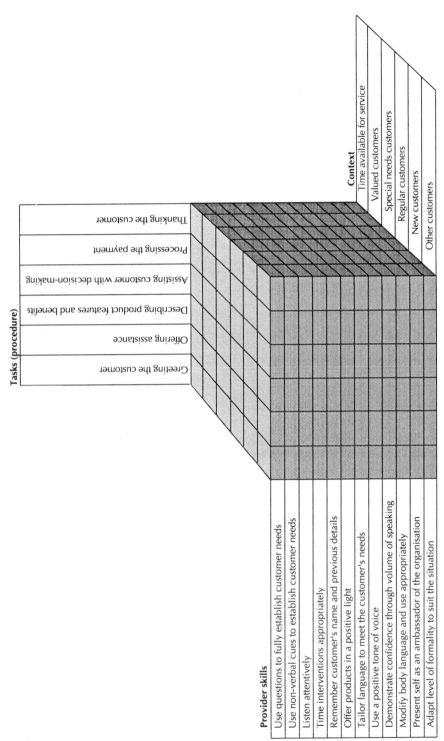

Figure 2.3   Procedure, skills and context for service

SUE DURMAN, of Killara, recovering from an operation and unable to get around, tells us she wanted a video of *Aladdin* for her daughter. She rang David Jones at Chatswood and asked if they could send a copy out. The video, they said, was too small for the delivery truck, but a staff member who lived at Lindfield would drop it in. On her day off, "an extremely delightful young lady" walked from her home at Lindfield to Killara to make the delivery.

(*SMH*, 11/8/94)

Three-dimensional approaches are hard to handle, so it is suggested that a two-dimensional approach is used for performance assessment, at the same time allowing for a range of contexts in which the tasks are performed. If the contexts are a varied and vital aspect of task performance, it is suggested that the two-dimensional matrix is retained and used in the same format for each of the contexts.

Further thoughts about the attributes for successful performance

Competency approaches thus look at two axes, the first being the task axis (consistent with the procedural dimension of the service model in chapter one), and the second being the attribute axis.

The attribute aspect of competence has been described by Gonczi, Hager and Oliver (1990, p. 1):

> The competence of professionals derives from their possessing a set of relevant attributes such as knowledge, abilities, skills and attitudes. These attributes which jointly underlie competence are often referred to as competencies. So a competency is a combination of attributes underlying some aspect of successful professional performance.

The key word here is 'combination'. Very seldom is a single attribute required in the performance of a task. Perhaps the difficulty that most trainers have with the definition and use of 'competency' rests with their desire to oversimplify, not only to the extent that the performance aspect is solely considered, but where attributes are applicable, to attempt to combine only one attribute with the performance of the task.

The performance by a hairdresser of cutting and styling could easily be subjected to a task analysis and broken down into tasks that need to be performed. In this case these tasks would form the basis of the task axis. Were a one-dimensional behavioural approach used, a long and detailed list could be devised. The limitations of this are immediately apparent. Despite a staff member's ability to perform all the behaviours on the checklist, the outcome could still be quite unsatisfactory for the client.

Adding the second dimension of attributes to the analysis provides the opportunity for one to consider attributes such as a knowledge of hair types and styles, judgement of the most appropriate style to suit the customer's needs, and the ability to communicate with the client before, during and after the session. The last of these attributes would be a key aspect of a successful performance and could not be ticked off the checklist as 'Was the customer asked what he or she wanted?' Throughout the cutting and styling process, complex combinations of communication skills, problem-solving, judgement and psychomotor skill work together to produce a satisfactory outcome. In order to assess competence, we therefore need to do more than pay lip-service to the complexity of human activity. Systematic analysis of the attributes which underpin excellent outcomes of service provision can assist in the development of more appropriate assessment and appraisal methods. A competent hairdresser is thus one who is able to perform a wide range of tasks using complex combinations of attributes.

Before attempting to analyse potential attributes that underlie performance of superior service provision in a systematic way, a further point must be made regarding assessment of competence. Many authors stress that competency-based training requires only the assessment of outcomes. A summative assessment of outcomes would, in the case of the hairdresser, show the cut to be a good one if judged to be so by the assessor, and if one is lucky, also by the client. However, it may be that the outcome resulted from luck; a happy coincidence (why do apprentice hairdressers always train on the curly-haired clients?). Further, an unsuccessful outcome could be the result of difficult circumstances, but the lack of success still attributed to poor performance. So, in assessing performance, a decision must be made as to whether processes and outcomes are important, or whether assessment of outcomes is all that necessary.

Chapter three will attempt to discuss these employee attributes in a systematic way, adding communication skills as one of the most important attributes that service staff bring to their encounters with customers. This will further assist with the development, in later chapters, of job descriptions that list the skills, knowledge and other attributes necessary for good job performance. Consideration of the complex combination of cognitive and communication skills relating to task performance gives the manager a basis on which to make a professional and holistic judgement of competence.

QUALITY SERVICE

Although, strictly speaking, 'quality' is a noun describing a degree of excellence, common usage implies 'good' or 'excellent' quality. Quality service meets and exceeds expectations of clients, and this is the meaning associated with the terms as they appear throughout this book.

Since customers define quality based on their perceptions, there is a need to bring these perceptions to front-line staff so that they perform competently in meeting customers' expectations. Hence the customer feedback loop, shown in Figure 2.4. Methods for closing this loop are many and varied, such as focus groups, surveys, customer feedback forms etc. These methods are usually handled in any marketing textbook. In many cases, the problem is that feedback relating to customer satisfaction is channelled towards senior management and reaches staff second- or third-hand (if at all). In assuring excellence in quality service, the feedback process needs to have front-line staff as its focus. These employees should seek feedback as part of their duties, recording and discussing the customers' input through meetings and debriefings. Where focus groups form the basis for this feedback, management can facilitate, but employees need to hear the customers' comments and suggestions first-hand. Responsiveness to customer needs and anticipation of

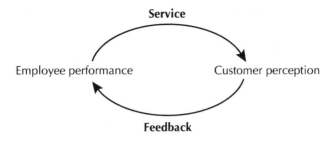

Figure 2.4   Customer feedback loop

consumer trends should be the preserve of front-line staff and not only of the Director of Marketing.

In order to evaluate the success (or otherwise) of service delivery, a useful technique is to devise some service dimensions for review and evaluation arising from discussions with staff and customers. In one such study, by students at the Northern Beaches College of TAFE, clear-cut differences between the expectations of customers visiting clubs and restaurants and others staying in hotels and budget accommodation were demonstrated. Two hundred and three people were interviewed in this unpublished research, and asked to rate the importance of the dimensions of quality, value, efficiency, friendliness, politeness, attentiveness to customer needs and guidance. The resultant ratings are presented in Figure 2.5.

The results showed significant differences with regard to quality of service expected in restaurants versus budget accommodation, although value for money was rated high for all four sectors. Also of note is the similarity in scores for friendliness. Clearly customers visiting all four sectors of the hospitality industry have similar expectations regarding friendliness, while not expecting the same levels of attentiveness.

In another exploratory study undertaken in the United States (Zeithaml, Parasuraman & Berry 1990), twelve focus group interviews were conducted, three in each of the following service sectors: retail banking; credit cards; securities brokerage; and product repair and maintenance. As a result of the research, ten dimensions of service quality emerged, as summarised in Figure 2.6.

Customer expectations are specific to one organisation. Thorough and ongoing research into these expectations and the customer satisfaction ratings, in relation to the service dimensions that are priorities for your customers, is essential in the process of managing human resources so that service training is focused on the achievement of customer satisfaction.

Evaluation of processes and outcomes

The processes and outcomes assessed in training and appraisals should be evaluated in terms of customer perception. Being customer-driven means that 'good' performance is not judged solely by management. Evaluation of service quality is something the customer does. The employee, in finding out directly what the customer needs and expects and how the customer has evaluated the service received, should then utilise this knowledge to develop and enhance his or her service strategies. The manager's role is to facilitate this learning.

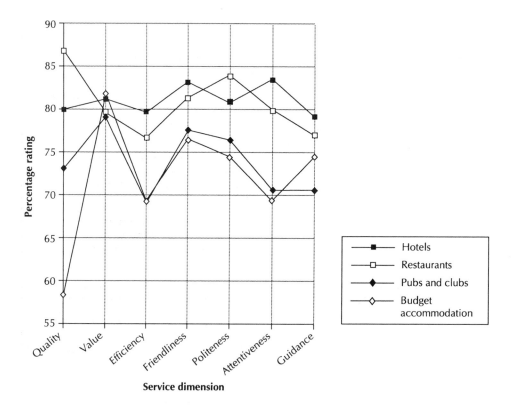

Figure 2.5   Ratings on service dimensions

Figure 2.6 Ten dimensions of service quality
(Source: Zeithamel, Parasuraman & Berry 1990, pp. 21, 22)

Dimension and Definition	Examples of Specific Questions Raised by Customers
Tangibles: Appearance of physical facilities, equipment, personnel, and communication materials.	Are the bank's facilities attractive? Is my stockbroker dressed appropriately? Is my credit card statement easy to understand? Do the tools used by the repair person look modern?
Reliability: Ability to perform the promised service dependably and accurately.	When a loan officer says he will call me back in 15 minutes, does he do so? Does the stockbroker follow my exact instructions to buy or sell? Is my credit card statement free of errors? Is my washing machine repaired right the first time?
Responsiveness: Willingness to help customers and provide prompt service.	When there is a problem with my bank statement, does the bank resolve the problem quickly? Is my stockbroker willing to answer any questions? Are charges for returned merchandise credited to my account promptly? Is the repair firm willing to give me a specific time when the repair person will show up?
Competence: Possession of the required skills and knowledge to perform the service.	Is the bank teller able to process my transactions without fumbling around? Does my brokerage firm have the research capabilities to accurately track market developments? When I call my credit card company, is the person at the other end able to answer my questions? Does the repair person appear to know what he is doing?
Courtesy: Politeness, respect, consideration, and friendliness of contact personnel.	Does the bank teller have a pleasant demeanor? Does my broker refrain from acting busy or being rude when I ask questions? Are the telephone operators in the credit card company consistently polite when answering my calls? Does the repair person take off his muddy shoes before stepping on my carpet?

Figure 2.6—*continued*

Dimension and Definition	Examples of Specific Questions Raised by Customers
Credibility: Trustworthiness, believability, honesty of the service provider.	Does the bank have a good reputation? Does my broker refrain from pressuring me to buy? Are the interest rates/fees charged by my credit card company consistent with the services provided? Does the repair firm guarantee its services?
Security: Freedom from danger, risk, or doubt.	Is it safe for me to use the bank's automatic teller machines? Does my brokerage firm know where my stock certificate is? Is my credit card safe from unauthorised use? Can I be confident that the repair job was done property?
Access: Approachability and ease of contact.	How easy is it for me to talk to senior bank officials when I have a problem? Is it easy to get through to my broker over the telephone? Does the credit card company have a 24-hour, toll-free telephone number? Is the repair service facility conveniently located?
Communication: Keeping customers informed in language they can understand and listening to them.	Can the loan officer explain clearly the various charges related to the mortgage loan? Does my broker avoid using technical jargon? When I call my credit card company, are they willing to listen to me? Does the repair firm call when they are unable to keep a scheduled repair appointment?
Understanding the Customer: Making the effort know customers and their needs.	Does someone in my bank recognise me as a regular customer? Does my broker try to determine what my specific financial objectives are? Is the credit limit set by my credit card company consistent with what I can afford (i.e., neither too high nor too low)? Is the repair firm willing to be flexible enough to accommodate *my* schedule?

EXERCISES AND DISCUSSION

1. Using the glossary at the back of this book, explain the following terms as you understand them.

    Competency
    Holistic assessment
    Recognition of prior learning
    Tasks
    Attributes

2. List some tasks performed by service personnel in a sector of your choice.

3. List some the attributes required by staff for giving good service in the sector you chose in question 2.

4. Draw a two-dimensional chart to illustrate the tasks and attributes from questions 2 and 3. Attempt to decide which attributes are necessary for which tasks (may involve more than one attribute).

5. How would you define quality service?

6. Review the two research studies of service and customer expectations. Which dimensions of service would you investigate if researching service in the medical profession?

3

COMMUNICATION IN THE SERVICE INTERACTION

SUMMARY

This chapter deals in detail with communication in relation to customer service. It demonstrates the high levels of performance that are required for complex and adaptable communication which is responsive to customer needs and to contextual factors.

CHAPTER OBJECTIVES

On completion of this chapter you will be able to:

- explain the importance of communication in service provision;
- differentiate between perception and inference;
- define communication competence;
- explain the effect of non-verbal communication in the service context by giving some examples;
- discuss whether training can enhance communication effectiveness.

COMMUNICATION IN THE SERVICE INTERACTION

A 'good attitude' is an expression that is frequently used in discussions about requirements for staff in the services sector. Owners and managers of organisations demand that staff have the 'right attitude' and job applicants are extolled to demonstrate a 'positive attitude' in the interview. Such a vague concept is difficult to grasp and utilise, and since the understanding of social psychology is not the aim of this book, an explanation in more specific terms of what is generally implied by a 'good attitude' towards customers, and what is generally meant by 'quality service' in terms of communication competence will be made.

Attitudes have generally been seen as orientations of the mind (O'Keefe 1990) and as predispositions for overt behaviour. Being highly intuitive, judging prospective and current employees on the basis of their attitudes is thus most difficult. The prospect of facing a tribunal in which discrimination has been charged and arguing that selection and promotion decisions were based on an evaluation of an employee's attitude would be hard to defend. Communication competence in the service context therefore needs to be addressed, to lead to more effective selection and training of service staff.

PERCEPTION

Customer, guest and client perceptions have been raised in the two preceding chapters, but the concept of perception requires further elaboration. It is the individual's basis for selecting and ordering, for developing a meaningful understanding of events and persons. Delia and Swanson (1976, p. 14) define perception in the following way: 'Perception is an active, constructive process, involving classification, interpretation and inference'.

Generally, persons of the same culture have the tendency to share interpretations, to have similar world views. The tendency for misunderstanding occurs where events and persons are perceived quite differently. Decisions relating to 'quality', then, are based on interpretation and inference relating to behaviours exhibited by service staff. Where these behaviours are at odds with cultural expectations, this can lead to evaluations of poor service. However, this is not always the case, since novelty has great appeal and the effect of the behaviour might be pleasing. Visitors from cultures where behaviour is influenced by formal codes of conduct might find it original and interesting to be dealt with in an informal manner. Yet others might find the same approach quite offensive. Despite common cultural expectations, these two different interpretations can be made.

Two aspects of this perceptual process (attending to only some dimensions of service, interpreting them in different ways and making inferences based on these interpretations), are worth noting. The first is that it is a dynamic process, with testing and adaptation of interpretations as the communication process unfolds. Second, each communication process is unique. The combined effects of verbal and non-verbal cues with their attendant responses would be impossible to reproduce in training exercises. At best, the service staff can be made more aware of customers' perceptions and encouraged to use reflection and discussion to develop alternate strategies for future use.

What, then, are the implications for service delivery? They are that:

- each individual has a unique world view;
- each individual pays attention to different things;
- each event or interaction with service staff can be interpreted differently by both staff member and customer;
- inferences are based on these interpretations.

From this, four inferences can be:

- the staff don't care;
- the staff don't know what they are doing;
- the staff are inefficient; or
- the staff are caring and capable.

Whether accurate or not, these inferences contribute substantially to consumer decision-making.

IT'S THE BUSIEST time of the tax year, with taxpayers struggling with returns, pay offices screaming for advice ... and the Australian Taxation Office chose yesterday to move its entire Hunter Street office, about 1,000 staff, to Hurstville. An office manager in Waterloo rang its inquiry number yesterday to get more group certificates, only to be told the number wasn't operating yet. Please call back today. It's a great way to run a railroad. The office is at 12–22 Woniora Road, phone 374 1200, if working.
(SMH, 5/7/94)

PERSUASION

In sales and service departments, attempts are made by staff to make intelligent and strategic decisions relating to communication in order to meet the needs of customers. This requires flexibility and perspective-taking, enabling the individual staff members to analyse and anticipate the needs of their customers and respond accordingly. It also demonstrates a high level of cognitive ability which is an integral part of communication competence.

As Delia and Swanson (1976, p. 33) say,

> The development of the ability to adapt communications, in turn, rests upon the acquisition of cultural knowledge and the capacity to understand the perspective's of others in communicative situations.

This idea of cultural perspective-taking is most valuable, and it rests on 'the acquisition of cultural knowledge'. Cultural knowledge as a useful basis for communication implies that learning about cultural differences or experiencing them is useful in the training of service staff. In recent times, the importance of knowledge has been downgraded, the focus being on skills and procedures. The implication here is that a knowledge of cultures could be a valuable criterion on which to base a selection decision. It does not imply, though, that an individual who knows a lot about another culture will use that knowledge appropriately, but it still is a more useful basis for staff selection and training than the global concepts of a 'good attitude' and 'attractive appearance'!

COMMUNICATION COMPETENCE

A new, applied communication perspective (Kaye 1992), known as 'adult communication management', crosses a number of theoretical boundaries to introduce valuable ideas for interpersonal communication.

> Essentially communication management refers to the ways in which communicating individuals construct, co-ordinate and clarify their meanings. There is also a suggestion here that if reciprocity occurs, that is to say, where individuals are acting toward and communicating with each other on the basis of mutually developed understandings, these individuals are displaying facets or some form of communication competence.
>
> (Kaye 1992, p. 6)

Kaye emphasises that communication is not a series of acts but a process, and that communication processes need to be understood in terms of the context in which they occur. (Contextual factors have already been described as they impact on the service encounter, further contributing to the complexity of the communication process.) Taking this one step further, Kaye suggests that communication competence may refer not only to the ability to relate to others, but also to the ability to shape and modify the context or environment in which communication occurs so that communication is optimised.

This approach—a systems approach—recognises that people can change the context for communication to enhance it. In providing a service, there are a number of ways in which this could be done, one being by changing the setting in which the interaction occurs. Moving out from behind a desk to assist someone is an example of an effort to facilitate communication. Recent changes to hotel reception desks, bank counters and restaurant seating plans are evidence of efforts to improve customer relations by making physical changes. Design elements of the system of communication can have dramatic effects, optimising or frustrating effective communication. Peters and Waterman, in their now-famous work *In Search of Excellence* (1982), sought to find factors that distinguished effective systems.

Seeking customer feedback was one such factor, with face-to-face discussions with customer groups and listening and responding to their needs. Systems with effective communication between staff, between departments, with customers and with suppliers are more likely to attain the level of quality service they seek to deliver. Egan (1988a) refers to communication as 'the lifeblood of organisations'.

Finally, communication competence does not reside in the behaviour exhibited by an individual, but in the *evaluation* of the appropriateness of that behaviour in that context: behaviour is not objectively appropriate or effective (Cooper 1991). Competency in communication (reciprocal construction of meaning) is ever-changing, given the perceptions of the individuals involved. This is particularly important to note, since managers and trainers are expected to judge frequently the effectiveness of interpersonal communication in the workplace. This introduces a third party into the perceptual process, for whom the meaning could be different to that shared between the customer and the staff member.

(Readers need not feel disheartened by the complexity of this process; as managers and trainers, your role is not to judge communication effectiveness so much as it is to encourage your employees to reflect and learn from experience. Facilitation of learning, particularly as it relates to the personal dimension of service, will be covered in detail in the later chapters on training.)

To illustrate communication misunderstanding, we need go no further than the trip to the hairdressers, where discussions about length, cut and style frequently lead to unanticipated outcomes and sometimes sheer horror. In this instance, the role of the hairdresser, as in most service positions, is to find out the customer's needs and expectations, and to fulfil them by following the appropriate procedures in cutting and styling. No matter how skilled a craftsperson, the hairdresser who does not communicate effectively with clients will lose business. Disappointment, shock and dismay at the results of a session at the hairdressers can put the salon's reputation at risk. The client, as well as never returning, will tell a number of others about the disaster. Despite how difficult it must be to be driven by client requests, the hairdresser cannot impose his or her own ideas of style. The exercise of the hairdresser's skill and craft is in fact severely limited by the desires of the clients.

In the case of sales positions, the customer's idea of good taste is often quite contrary to what one would expect:

'I run a wholesale import business, offering giftware and kitchenware. One of the first things I learnt about the business was that customers bought the most amazing things. Items that I thought were tasteful stayed in the warehouse and others (less tasteful) disappeared overnight. I tried asking my clients what they wanted, but they had little idea. In the end I had a range of samples made up and took to the streets asking for feedback. I also learned to ask, not "Do you like this?", but "Would you buy this and why/ why not?" '

This illustrates the different perceptions that the customer may have of the product's features and benefits. Procedures are an integral aspect of service; the importance of context, or system, in which communication occurs was mentioned earlier. Guests arriving at a hotel and accustomed to waiting in line for checking in would be pleasantly surprised by the porter taking them straight up to the room and completing registration forms there. This change to the procedure (and hence perception) enhances and improves communication effectiveness between front-line staff and their customers, allowing for the development of convivial relationships at a personal level.

In the banking sector, bullet-proof glass inhibits communication; but the introduction of desks for tellers enhances the comfort of both staff and customers, especially important where the majority of bank transactions often occur with the customer standing at an automatic teller machine.

NON-VERBAL COMMUNICATION

A chapter on communication would not be complete without some discussion on non-verbal communication in the service encounter. Various aspects are described below, with some examples.

Body language

Facial expression, posture, gestures and eye contact are well-known aspects of body language. They indicate a degree of interest and attentiveness which is displayed towards another person.

Timing

Timing, a non-verbal form of communication, should be subject to more research in the service sector. It is an essential aspect of service: some customers want immediate attention while others want to be left alone. Should the staff member intervene, or leave them alone? If a number of customers are waiting, who should be served first?

Food service in a restaurant is a good example of the importance of timing. Research has shown that attentiveness is more important at the start of a meal than at the end. Delays in serving dessert and coffee are generally acceptable; similar waiting periods are unacceptable when the customer first arrives. If one were to look at this and attempt to optimise the timing between interventions, the outcome may look like this:

Greeting and seating	1 minute after arrival
Offering the menu	2–3 minutes later
Taking drinks orders	At the time of menu presentation
Delivering drinks orders	10 minutes later
Taking meal orders	At the time of drink service
Delivering meal orders	20 minutes later
Checking all is satisfactory	5 minutes later
Clearing table	5–10 minutes after finishing eating
Bringing desert menu	5–10 minutes later
Serving desert and coffee	15 minutes later
Clearing and presenting bill	10 minutes later
Processing payment	5 minutes.

This process, in total, may take approximately ninety minutes. (Of course, if a customer only has an hour's lunch break, the timing would have to be faster.) A customer's needs and the style of service, the type of menu, and so on, are all factors in the timing of service. Being hungry would change a person's perception. For a relaxed dinner meal, people might like service a little slower. These are differences which need to be taken into account in the development of the menu and the resulting procedures required for service. The optimum timing is generally a management decision based on the type of restaurant and its clientele.

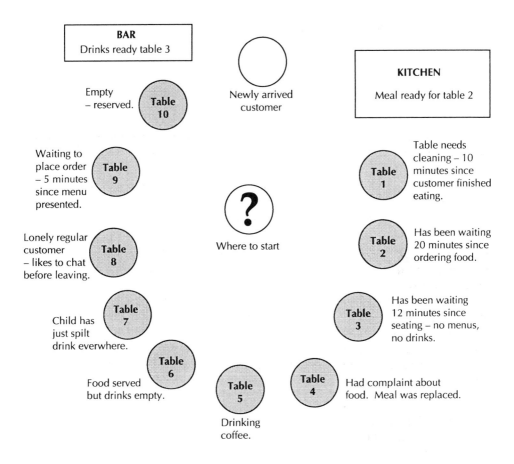

Figure 3.1   Managing tasks – timing in service delivery

From the viewpoint of the front-line staff, this is simplistic to say the least. Each customer has different needs, and sometimes the same customer has different needs on different days. These needs all relate to timing which, if not appropriate, might lead to the assessment by the customer that the service is poor. Timing in this context is a communication factor. The customer infers from the speed of service that the staff have a poor attitude and that service is bad.

So far the focus has been on only one customer and the dilemmas raised as to optimum timing for service intervention in this situation. Add to this a number of other customers, all at different stages of the meal, and a chef in the kitchen preparing hot food (as in Figure 3.1). The synchronisation required is an extraordinary effort, requiring cognitive skills at a high level. The waiter carrying plates through the restaurant who seems able to avoid eye-contact (this is a non-verbal contract—'I know you are distressed, and should serve you, but don't have time and better not acknowledge you until I can deal with your concerns') is, consciously or not, using spontaneous, high-level decision-making. What strategy could be chosen for dealing with the customers in Figure 3.1, given the problem of priority it presents?

Voice qualities

Voice qualities (such as the tone of voice, speech rate and volume) also contribute to inferences made by listeners. Talking fast might lead to the inference that the person is busy and not really interested, while a softly spoken suggestion may lead to the inference that the salesperson lacks confidence in the product.

Use of space

One of the most interesting uses of space in the retail field is the supermarket rumoured to leave boxes in the aisles as a deliberate policy, to infer that turnover is so high that they can't keep up with the pace, and that this turnover results from low pricing. This is a deliberate effort to influence customer perception of value for money, and raises images of customers with their supermarket trolleys fighting their way past hold-ups where staff are unpacking boxes. Glorious wide aisles, shelf-packing outside opening times, good lighting and other features, in direct contrast to the above supermarket, lead to perceptions (whether true or not) of high overheads and less value for money.

Spaciousness has always featured in fine dining restaurants and hotel suites: using space to create ambience is a critical design factor, contributing to the customers' perceptions relating to atmosphere.

Use of artefacts

Another aspect of the decor is the use of artefacts, fittings and artworks to add further to the ambience. One Great Barrier Reef resort has invested enormous amounts of money in the artwork on display and is frequently featured in the media. The message that this is an exclusive and expensive resort, unlikely to have children in residence, is no doubt being communicated to potential guests.

LISTENING

Listening would have to be the most underrated skill in the service industry. Two aspects of listening skills are the ability to accurately discern information from another person, and the ability to support the communication process, through attentiveness and involvement. Dwyer (1993) has differentiated listening into attending listening, encouraging listening, reflecting listening and active listening. Better listening (attending listening) translates directly into finding out exactly what the customer is looking for and expects. Better encouraging and reflecting listening translates into time saved by not talking about product features and benefits that are of no interest to the customer. Better listening translates into time saved by both customers and staff. Better listening enables faster and more effective problem-solving. Better listening results in more sales and more profit.

If asked to list the criteria on which to base selection decisions, listening competence should be at the top of the list. It is one ability directly relevant to sales and service, and an evaluation of an individual's listening skills increases the validity of the selection decision. The interview is an ideal situation in which to test an applicant's listening skills, and yet this is seldom done.

ASSUMPTIONS

Although communication is a complex process and difficult by its very nature to analyse, its importance in customer relations has long been recognised. For the purposes of this book, in developing successful strategies for recruitment, selection, training and appraisal of service personnel, the following assumptions are made.

Creative thinking as the basis for service interactions
Creative thinking forms the basis for many interpersonal communications when flexibility and adaptability are exhibited.

Levels of communication competence
There are levels of communication competence that could be based on perspective-taking and adaptability, as well as other factors such as linguistic skill.

Development of communication competence
Communication can be improved by the development of a wide range of knowledge, ideas or constructs, to form the basis for analysis and interpretation of interpersonal behaviour.

Adult learning processes
Communication skills can be enhanced through experience, where this experience is utilised in a learning process to further develop ideas and/or constructs about human behaviour and motivation.

Creative thinking in interpersonal service communication
Creative thinking in communication involves the synthesis of known constructs or ideas with their extension to new situations in which they are evaluated appropriate or inappropriate.

DESCRIBING SERVICE COMMUNICATION COMPETENCE

To use these assumptions to develop criteria for selection, for training and for appraising staff performance, the now widely used approach of writing instructional objectives (known as the Bloom Taxonomy) is extended to encompass communication. It will be further extended in later chapters to assist in the planning of criterion-referenced approaches to human resource development. Essentially, the competency approach is based on criterion-referenced assessment, and this approach will here form the basis for strategies in training front-line staff.

In 1948 a committee of the American Psychological Society devised three areas into which instructional objectives could be classified: the cognitive domain; the psychomotor domain; and the affective domain. The cognitive domain then subdivided into knowledge, comprehension, application, analysis, synthesis and evaluation; the psychomotor domain into perception, set, guided response, mechanism, complex overt response, adaptation and origination. Despite a lack of empirical support, the Bloom Taxonomy of the cognitive domain has been widely used in human resource management due to its practical value in devising assessment methods and evaluating human performance.

The main attributes of human performance are fine motor co-ordination, thinking and reasoning, and advanced communication skill. For this reason, these form the basis for the following adaptation of the Bloom Taxonomy.

Psychomotor domain

The psychomotor domain deals with physical skills and the levels of application of those skills to tasks (the levels are modifications of those used by Bloom and his associates). Physical actions form part of many procedural tasks, such as carrying several plates simultaneously or driving a tour bus whilst commenting on the scenery.

Cognitive domain

The cognitive domain deals with thinking. Following the above tour bus example, the cognitive processes involved in concentrating on road conditions and making decisions to slow or accelerate, change gears, replace the music tape and mention a passing feature and its history are all part of the cognitive processing of the driver. As a tourist on board, one would have some concern that the driver was faced with cognitive overload!

Communication domain

The communication domain (added to the Bloom Taxonomy) assists with descriptions of the levels of communication competence. These levels have no empirical basis whatsoever, and are offered simply for the practical value they might have in the field of customer relations training.

In the example of the tour bus driver, group harmony would need to be achieved in the tour group. Having read the suggested levels of the communication domain, you might like to speculate on the level of communication necessary in achieving harmony among the group of tourists, and compare that to Figure 3.2.

Communication is an integral and complex process and does not operate in a vacuum. It is based on personal construct systems and thus cannot be viewed as independent of cognitive processes. Constructivist theory suggests that 'people use their interpersonal construct systems to attribute meaning to the behaviour and communication of others' (Kaye 1992, p. 13). As the reciprocal construction of meaning relies on both verbal and non-verbal factors, communication requires perspective-taking. Added to one's own perception is speculation of the other person's perceptions and attributions. From this, strategies for behaviour (in this case communication) are developed and chosen if appropriate. This is often an instantaneous and unconscious decision occurring in the present, based on past experience, and predicting future outcomes.

Thus, the cognitive and communication processes are inexorably linked. Since non-verbal cues play a large part in communicating and interpreting meaning, and as many of these cues have a basis in the psychomotor process, all three process domains are often linked together. The levels suggested for communication are as follows.

Ritual communication
The ritual level would include socially appropriate communication (such as speaking to people, or acceptable formats and wording for simple letter writing) and other repetitive social contexts. In the context of service, this could include the choice of appropriate words, tone, posture and timing in the greeting of a customer.

Routine communication
Routine communication includes that which occurs frequently and requires little perspective-taking or adaptation, such as taking bookings.

Modified communication
Strategies chosen for modifying communication would require consideration of contextual factors and perspective-taking. At this level, communication would be modified following an evaluation of time available, customer non-verbal cues and perspective-taking in relation to the needs expressed by customers.

Complex, modified communication
Suggested for the complex, modified level of communication are a wide range of personal constructs and strategies requiring application in novel situations and taking the other person(s) into consideration. Problem-solving and complaint handling are good examples of complex, modified communication, requiring that unique and appropriate solutions are found to unique problems.

Complex, modified, abstract communication
Constructs and strategies are applied to highly complex contexts at a level that require abstract thinking and communication relating to these abstract concepts. Marketing a service entails selling abstract ideas to potential customers and dealing with the image of the organisation in the eyes of the public.

Originative communication
Reasoned judgement, using highly developed language skills to express interaction between concrete objects or experience and abstract thought, would exemplify

originative communication; that is, communicating abstract ideas based on critical thinking processes. Research and development of theories relating to service delivery, and the communication of these to an audience, would indicate success at this level.

Pragmatically, these levels are only useful where they enable managers to look at tasks and procedures and decide upon the levels of psychomotor skill, cognitive thinking and communication skill necessary for successful performance. The value of this approach is immediately evident in realising that quality service entails high levels of performance in all three domains. Cognitive skills demonstrated in the analysis of situations, combined with adaptive communication are clearly essential requirements in providing quality service. Service positions have traditionally been filled by untrained personnel. The argument presented here is that, contrary to the belief that it is easy to provide quality service, the skill levels required are high on the scale of difficulty. Although appearing intuitive

Attribute axis

Task axis (driver)	Psychomotor domain (doing)						Cognitive domain (thinking)						Communication domain (communicating)				
	Guided response	Mechanical response	Complex response	Adaptive response	Original response	Creative complex response	Recall	Comprehension	Application	Analysis	Synthesis	Evaluation	Routine communication	Modified communication	Complex, modified communication	Complex, modified, abstract communication	Originative communication
Greeting tourists							X						X				
Stowing baggage		X							X								
Changing gears			X						X								
Overtaking				X					X								
Commentating									X							X	
Developing camaraderie										X						X	
Handling problems												X				X	

Figure 3.2 Performance domains (after Bloom & Associates, 1974)

('salespeople are born, not made'), it is argued here that having come to grips with the attributes required for the performance of service tasks, managers can ensure that strategies for the development of their staff can further assist with the promotion of competence in providing quality service.

Chapters one, two and three have set the scene for developing strategies for employing and training personnel to provide quality service. The concept of competent performance, perceived as such by customers and managers, will emerge again in the subsequent chapters that will deal with recruitment, selection and training. All human resource practices suggested will be based on the model of quality service and on the discussion of communication competence in this chapter. In particular, these suggestions will be based on the assumptions made earlier in the chapter about the role of creative thinking in the communication process and the development of communication competence where experiential learning forms the basis for this learning.

EXERCISES AND DISCUSSION

1. How do you feel about the description of competent service staff as those having the right 'attitude'?

2. Having experienced service in a variety of contexts (supermarkets, restaurants, banks and surgeries), explain how much time was spent waiting during the phases of your visit and the inferences you made about the use of time.

3. While visiting these venues, describe the impact that objects, uniforms and other artefacts had on you.

4. Critique the levels of communication competence.

5. Explain whether communication competence can be enhanced through training.

4

HUMAN RESOURCE PLANNING

SUMMARY

This chapter deals with job descriptions (the tasks to be performed by service staff) and job specifications (the attributes they need to perform these tasks well). Both are used as the basis for advertising for new staff and for selecting the best candidates. Good selection decisions ensure that both the procedural and personal dimensions of service provide the basis on which selection criteria are chosen and decisions are made.

CHAPTER OBJECTIVES

On completion of this chapter you will be able to:

- write a job description with a service focus;
- decide on selection criteria which are directly relevant to customer service;
- develop a detailed job specification;
- enhance existing job descriptions and specifications which show only the procedural dimension of service.

HUMAN RESOURCE PLANNING

Human resource planning and review are core principles of quality management. Having developed organisational objectives, the next step for management is to ensure that an adequate number of trained and motivated staff are available to meet defined service standards.

Important managerial considerations are the number of full-time and part-time staff to be employed in the organisation. The service industry is notorious for the large number of part-time and casual staff it employs and for its high labour turnover. This is at a high cost: simply recruiting, selecting and training new staff is an expensive exercise. Depending upon the seniority of the person employed, the cost

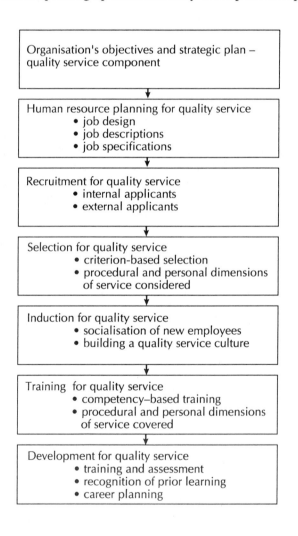

Figure 4.1 Human resource planning

is estimated to be 10–15 per cent of annual pay; if the company experiences a 20 per cent annual turnover, this is an unexpectedly large sum of money. In the services sector, staff turnover is generally very high and 20 per cent is a conservative figure. Many organisations have turnover rates of over 100 per cent, as the front-line, casual staff changes over many times in the course of a year. (See chapter fourteen for a full discussion on staff turnover.) Even where the cost of recruiting and training casual staff is fairly low (but it is always higher than one would expect), the cost that is not calculated is the irreparable damage done to customer relations by poor service delivered by staff who are unsuitable or untrained. Thus, loss of business caused by poor service is another factor in the calculation of the effects of poor staffing and training practices. Finally, the last potential cost for organisations is the cost of litigation if an employee claims discrimination, sexual harassment or unfair dismissal. Good employment practices, the careful selection of staff on valid criteria, thorough employee induction, the establishment of rules and procedures, good training and ongoing performance appraisal all contribute to employee and customer satisfaction, and to increased profits, and can also reduce costs where there is a risk of litigation brought by dissatisfied customers or staff.

'A student of mine recently described to me how she had left the ailing rag trade to open her own restaurant in North Sydney. Her decision to do so was based on the fact that her friends and family were most complimentary about her culinary skills. Having equipped the restaurant in a modest fashion on a small budget, her first step was to distribute leaflets to the local neighbourhood offering a discount on the opening night. With a seating capacity of seventy, the queue outside the door ensured that they would be bursting at the seams. Inside panic prevailed, since there were only two staff, the owner serving and her sister cooking. Unable to even open a bottle of wine, she describes the evening as an unforgettable disaster, with most customers leaving in disgust with the remainder complaining bitterly about the level of service. Over the years she employed a number of skilled hospitality staff who taught her all she needed to know, and with their help is now running a very successful enterprise. Many of these staff are still with the restaurant, and it is to them she owes much of the success of her operation.'

Having trained staff on hand at the right times is no easy task. Overstaffing can lead to budget blowout, while understaffing adds to staff stress levels, and can contribute to both customer and staff dissatisfaction. Many employers tackle this problem by employing casual staff who are more flexible in their working hours. Unfortunately, casual employees tend to lack commitment, which is mirrored by their employer's lack of commitment to their job security and career development. A high dependence on casual staff coupled with high labour turnover is a guarantee of low standards of quality. Investment in developing highly committed, well-trained and motivated staff pays dividends in the end by raising service standards, and ensuring consistency.

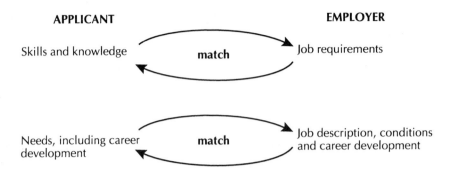

Figure 4.2 Match between job factors and applicant needs

JOB ANALYSIS

There are four facets to job analysis: job descriptions, job specifications, job design and job evaluation. The first of these, the job description, defines the role of the person, the duties and responsibilities of the individual in that job. This is very useful for employing and training staff: it ensures that the job applicant has a clear idea of what is expected of them, and that training meets any deficiencies an employee may have in relation to those duties. It avoids the development of unrealistic expectations of the role and consequent frustration, resulting in a higher than necessary number of resignations. One has to bear in mind that the recruitment and selection process aims to find a match between individual and organisational needs. This is, however, only half the equation. The second aim is to find a match between what the organisation has to offer and the individual's career needs (see Figure 4.2). Successful placement, by necessity, involves the employment of competent individuals who will find that their positions meet their expectations and fulfil their needs for further development.

Furthermore, the job description can be most useful should disciplinary procedures be implemented (see chapter thirteen). Where the job description has been issued and discussed in detail with the staff member, and where it forms a part of the training process, the employer can be fairly well assured that claims for unfair dismissal on the basis of unclear expectations are unlikely.

The second facet of job analysis is the development of a job specification, otherwise known as a person specification. This helps to define the skills, knowledge and experience necessary for individuals to perform the duties defined in the job description. Care should be taken in the writing of job specifications so as not to breach guidelines for equal employment opportunity (EEO), which is employment based on merit. Discrimination should not occur on any criterion which is not directly related to performance of the duties of the position. The more obvious criteria are age, sex, marital status and the like, and all are clearly spelt out in anti-discrimination legislation. There are forms of discrimination that occur, sometimes unthinkingly, which are not based on sound factors. Place of residence is one of these: employers decide on the applicant's behalf that 'it is too far to travel'. This is not the employer's decision, but that of the person applying for the job. If someone is willing to travel the required distance and time, this is no concern for an employer unless the employee is likely to be needed at short notice. Another example is the basis of 'need'. Having a dependant family can result in employers deciding to employ on the basis of financial need, while others decide that the children are a liability, likely to cause absenteeism. Non-parents on the other hand, are 'flighty and unstable'. None of these impressions are relevant to the employment decision, which should be based entirely on the skills, knowledge and experience the applicant has for the position. The development of a good job or person specification, with the communication skills required for customer service, can go a long way towards making sound, defensible decisions in the selection process.

The third facet of job analysis is job design. Multiskilling, or the performance of a wide range of tasks, is currently fashionable, making staff more flexible and versatile. Where this adds to job satisfaction it is most appropriate, enabling staff members to develop skills in a wide range of tasks. The only time when the addition of extra tasks is not appropriate is where staff find the routine duties performed easy to manage and have no desire to diversify. The addition of more routine or boring tasks simply causes frustration and dissatisfaction. Careful analysis of the needs of staff needs to be done when job design factors are considered. Not all staff look to their employment for career development and enrichment; some use their jobs and the money they earn as a means to other ends.

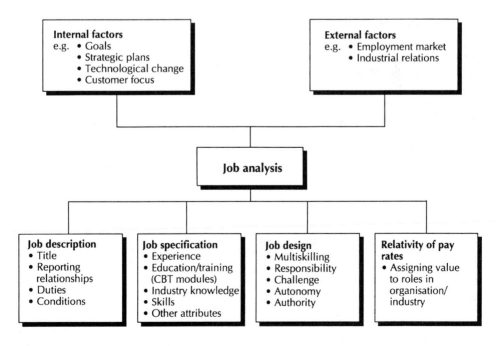

Figure 4.3 Process of job analysis

Job evaluation is the final facet of job analysis: decisions regarding the remuneration paid to a person in the position being based on the responsibility of that position in relation to others in the organisation. In doing so, a framework is created in which pay is matched to the level of skill required, with relativity between positions necessary from one department or employment stream to another in order to achieve equity.

JOB DESCRIPTIONS

In organisations of all sizes, job descriptions are valuable tools used to define the tasks, relationships and accountability of staff. They are the result of careful task analysis which defines key performance areas. In the services sector this is fairly difficult since many tasks are non-routine. The result is that many job descriptions poorly reflect the major areas of responsibility. In most job descriptions, like the task-oriented one shown over the page, only the routine, procedural aspects of job performance are covered. Following an earlier theme of two-dimensional service, these tasks are the more objective aspects of the job; tasks that can be easily observed and recorded are the more scientific aspects of the service role. If, however, there is an art to the delivery of effective customer service, there needs to be an attempt to define these aspects of the job in the job description. Many of these aspects form part of the personal dimension of service and relate to communication processes as they occur in the service interaction. The difficulty is that every situation is different: the customer is different, the questions they ask are different, the timing is different, the degree of importance of the interaction is different and so it goes on. An attempt must be made in the writing of job descriptions to reflect this, otherwise the job description has a tendency to list routine tasks that are rarely performed and form only a small part of what the employee does. The second, service-oriented job description attempts to reflect more accurately both the procedural and personal aspects of service delivery.

While task analysis is useful in yielding the procedures generally followed in performing routine tasks, another technique, the critical incident analysis, can be most useful in helping to define the more important non-routine but essential tasks that form part of quality service. Here, in the second, improved job description for a salesperson, the inclusion of the tasks 'engage in conversation where appropriate' and 'offer information and services where appropriate and where time allows' are examples of this. Calling a taxi for an elderly person struggling with parcels and helping them to the door, entertaining bored children while their parents reach decisions, or discussing family news and the weather are things that salespeople do all the time. These are part of what the customer calls a 'positive attitude'. This value-added service cannot be offered during periods when other customers are waiting, but it is these small things that are a 'service' and rate very highly in the customer's perception.

As can be seen in the second job description, the more frequent activities of the salesperson are listed first with other, less frequently performed tasks (such as checking stock levels) listed towards the end.

TASK-ORIENTED JOB DESCRIPTION

POSITION TITLE: Salesperson

REPORTS TO: Sales Manager

DEPARTMENT: Duty Free

JOB SUMMARY:

To determine customer purchase needs and to sell them the appropriate goods through explanation, demonstration and persuasion.

DUTIES:

Check stock levels
Organise stock transfers to other stores
Arrange stock and maintain cleanliness
Develop knowledge of new products
Demonstrate equipment where necessary
Explain product attributes to customers
Accept payment and process accurately, following store procedures
Operate point of sale terminal/cash register
Report daily sales
Maintain security

CONDITIONS OF SERVICE:

Shift work, Saturday and Sunday

Uses for job descriptions

Job descriptions, as mentioned before, are a valuable aid in the processes of recruiting, selection, induction, training and appraisal. They help to attract the right people to the organisation when used as the basis for describing jobs in advertisements; they can used to describe the duties in detail to job applicants at the interview; they can help clarify responsibilities and relationships at induction; they can be useful in training by allowing for the analysis of training needs; and they are referred to in the appraisal process, particularly when the staff member's performance is unsatisfactory.

The job description should include any of the following elements, providing they are relevant:

Job title	the title of the position
Department or location	the department or branch of the organisation where the job is located
Reports to	title of supervisor

SERVICE-ORIENTED JOB DESCRIPTION

POSITION TITLE: Salesperson

DEPARTMENT: Duty Free

REPORTS TO: Store Manager

JOB SUMMARY:

To determine customer purchase needs and to sell them the appropriate goods through explanation, demonstration and persuasion.

DUTIES:

Greet/acknowledge customers
Ask customers how assistance can be offered
Ask questions relating to purchases
Listen to customer requests
Attend to customer non-verbal communication cues, such as timing, use of
  space, eye contact, voice intonation
Time interventions appropriately
Suggest alternatives to meet customer needs in terms of product features
  and benefits
Request confirmation that needs are met by products suggested
Utilise open and closed questions as appropriate
Investigate if customer's requests for more information cannot be met, or if
  products are not currently available
Match product features or benefits to customer needs
Demonstrate equipment where necessary
Explain product attributes to customers
Gain commitment
Close sales
Accept payment and process accurately, following store procedures
Operate point of sale terminal/cash register
Arrange follow-up or apologise if unable to assist
Engage in conversation where appropriate and where time allows
Offer information and services where appropriate and where time allows
Seek feedback on products and service dimensions
Handle product and service complaints
Thank customers
Invite customers to return
Check stock levels
Organise stock transfers to other stores
Arrange stock and maintain cleanliness
Develop knowledge of new products
Report daily sales
Maintain security

Supervises	title(s) of subordinates, where applicable
Job summary	short summary of main duties
Duties	detailed list of duties, regular and occasional, each starting with an action verb
Responsibilities	list of any responsibilities, such as for money or equipment, where applicable
Lines of communication	necessary lines of communication to be developed outside the department, where applicable
Physical demands	any physical demands of the job, such as lifting, where applicable
Conditions of service	conditions, including such things as salary or wage and fringe benefits.

JOB SPECIFICATIONS

Otherwise known as 'a person specification', a job specification describes the ideal applicant. As mentioned earlier, this document is the basis on which the selection decision is made. The development of such a specification clarifies assumptions and ensures objectivity in the selection process. Not only does it avoid a breach of anti-discrimination legislation, it also ensures that staff are chosen for the contribution they can make to the achievement of the organisation's goals. In terms of competency-based human resource management, the job specification defines the personal attributes that are needed for the performance of tasks. These include knowledge, experience, and skills.

Looking at job specifications which were developed some years ago one might see attributes such as: appearance, attainments (education and experience), intelligence, interests (social and recreational activities), disposition (personality), circumstances (personal circumstances, supportive dependants), biographical details (age and proximity to work), values (will their views cause conflict?), financial situation (require income, accumulated assets?) and health (fitness and sporting activities). Without wishing to deal with each of these individually, the inappropriateness of questions based on these attributes is clear. Not only do they breach privacy guidelines, but most clearly have no relevance to performance at work. Of the ten attributes listed, only education and experience have direct relevance to future employment, and these, along with other criteria, should to be expanded to develop a list of valid attributes or factors that can be taken into account when choosing the best person for the job.

When choosing criteria on which to base the selection decision, they need to be listed in order of importance, or weighted. You might have noticed that the list of previous attributes started with 'appearance'.

'A careers adviser who recently came to talk to some young people about work in the service industry told them that rather than a long resume, they should send in a large glossy photograph and their name and address. I was outraged. The pressures brought to bear on young people to meet unrealistic ideals is absurd—enough of this happens on television and in magazines—and to also have most of the kids walk away deciding that they would never make it on the basis of a photograph was most damaging. Not everyone can look like a model; this is not what good customer service is about. I am sick of glamorous and useless employees standing around when I want someone I can talk to about what I need.'

A job specification is used to describe the best person suited to the position described in the job description. Some parts of the job specification are easily validated and provide a reasonably accurate assessment of applicant's potential for the job. An example would be the need for formal educational requirements that relate closely to the work to be carried out, such as a trade certificate. Other parts are intangible and very difficult to assess. Many advertisements require that applicants have 'a pleasant personality'. How does an interviewer assess personality with any objectivity? And how valid is an assessment of personality to the long-term performance of the individual on the job? On the other hand, surely 'personality' or 'attitude' is everything in the service industry? It may be, but 'personality' is not sufficiently specific. Instead, one needs to break a vague and subjective concept down into specific skills that are relevant to the job. Communication skills are a useful example: verbal communication, such as volume and clarity of speech, can be assessed with a far greater degree of accuracy, as can non-verbal and listening skills.

An interviewer with an appropriate checklist can look at things such as attentiveness, eye contact, facial expression, posture and can more easily predict the applicant's performance in the position than through a discussion of their family's origins. The worst interviewers ask totally inappropriate questions such as 'What sort of music do you like?', 'What do you do in your spare time?' and, at the very worst, 'Tell me about yourself'.

Experience

Work experience in relevant fields is clearly one of the most relevant aspects of the applicant's background and needs to be explored in some detail. This can be done in three ways. First, by asking about the tasks that the person has performed in previous jobs. These questions need to be carefully phrased, as closed questions will generally be answered in the affirmative with no clarification whatsoever. Applicants are known to exaggerate their skills and experience with the hope of finding employment. Second, the person's skills can be tested—a far more valid basis on which to select staff, and need not be time consuming.

'I am reminded of an employer who couldn't find good staff for his telephone sales business. He used to interview them all, but found that many left or were unsuitable. I suggested that he listen more carefully when they called up in response to the advertisement, and ask a few more questions in order to rate their communication and listening skills. Then I suggested that he ask the person to think about the features and benefits of a product, such as a toothbrush, and then call him back and attempt to sell one to him. Apparently he was delighted with the results of his new selection process.'

The last way in which skills and experience can be validated is by checking references with previous employers, asking specifically about procedures followed and problem-solving skills.

Applicants with no industry experience should be given the opportunity to examine their backgrounds for evidence of voluntary work that is relevant to their future employment. Service in the community is an oft-forgotten and valuable part of an individual's background, likely to have stimulated an interest in employment in a service position.

Education and training

Education is particularly relevant if there is a direct correlation between the studies undertaken and the work performed on the job. All too often service personnel are chosen on the basis of their academic results. Make no mistake: high levels of performance are good indicators of application and diligence, thinking and problem-solving, but academic performance alone is not a good indicator of future success in a people-oriented industry. Further evidence is necessary to establish that the applicant also has customer relations skills or potential.

Clearly, vocational training is directly relevant, and this is definitely the case where training is competency-based. If so, the applicant should have the competency outline and achievements recorded against industry standards. This is most valuable for the detail it provides, but it is useful to explore the context in which these assessments were made. In training and education, it is very difficult to simulate real-life pressures and the complexity of dealing with multiple customers simultaneously. These industry-developed competencies are generally procedurally based, leaving the personal and problem-solving aspects of quality service to be addressed. Again, some questions relating to matching service to customer needs should be included in the interview.

Communication skills

The personal dimension of service and the communication competencies necessary for the attainment of customer satisfaction were discussed in detail in chapter three. The levels of communication competence suggested could form the basis for a skills outline such as the one shown in Figure 3.2. Competency-based assessment and appraisal systems should be criterion-based—in other words, the individual's performance is compared to pre-established criteria. In the following skills chart, some important criteria have been listed and guidelines given, against which interviewers can evaluate skills that are relevant to customer service, either through observation during the interview or by asking appropriate questions. Planning the interview questions before the interview will be discussed in the next chapter, and these are based on the job specification.

Other skills and attributes

A number of other skills and attributes are listed in the following assessment chart, such as planning, problem-solving, assertiveness and stress management. This chart is criterion-referenced, giving guidelines on which selection can be based. It is essential that the criteria chosen clearly reflect the knowledge, skills and other attributes essential for successful performance in both the procedural and personal dimensions of service.

EXERCISES AND DISCUSSION

1. Develop a job description for a waiter or a bank teller.

2. List the reasons why a job description is useful.

3. Explain what a job specification is used for and why it is useful.

4. List some of the personal attributes you think are relevant for someone working in an historical theme park.

5. An old-fashioned manager remembers the days when ...

> you could advertise for exactly who you wanted.
> an agreement was an informal arrangement that suited the management.
> organisation charts were the right way up.
> not everyone wanted to be the general manager from day one.
> a system was a way of doing things.
> backing up meant reversing the company vehicle.
> senior staff didn't have to know where the letters were on a keyboard.
> you could handle the amount of information you were given.
> you could fire anyone you wanted to.
> you weren't expected to leave your office.
> there were multiple layers of supervisors and managers to protect you from the customers.

Comment on his remarks, contrasting current human resource management practices with those of the past.

SKILL ASSESSMENT CHART

INTERPERSONAL COMMUNICATION SKILLS

Initiative

Does not initiate interaction, does not respond adequately to requests for information.	Responds to requests, giving full information.	Initiates interaction, positive and outgoing, giving all necessary information with enthusiasm.

Tick appropriate box

[　]　　　　[　]　　　　[　]　　　　[　]　　　　[　]

Verbal communication skills

Expresses ideas adequately but needs to develop skill in attaining and maintaining receiver attention. Could improve with variety in vocal presentation and wider vocabulary.	Unable to express ideas verbally, poor vocabulary, monotonous tone, mumbles, uses 'ums'.	Communicates clearly and concisely to individuals or groups, maintaining interest and achieving objective of mutual understanding. Wide vocabulary. Voice qualities offer variety and express enthusiasm

Tick appropriate box

[　]　　　　[　]　　　　[　]　　　　[　]　　　　[　]

Non-verbal communication skills

Does not use body language consistent with verbal message	Uses body language consistently.	Uses non-verbal skills, e.g. gestures, facial expression and visual aids, to reinforce messages successfully and attain receiver's interests and understanding.

Tick appropriate box

[　]　　　　[　]　　　　[　]　　　　[　]　　　　[　]

Personal appearance

Dress and grooming inappropriate.	Presentation satisfactory.	Polished and professional presentation enhances image.

Tick appropriate box

[　]　　　　[　]　　　　[　]　　　　[　]　　　　[　]

© 1994 Van der Wagen Consulting Pty Ltd.

Listening skills

| Interrupts, offers solutions before problem expressed. | Shows empathy but needs to use feedback and questioning techniques further. Offers solutions too readily. | Uses body language feedback and questions to fully grasp the sender's message. |

Tick appropriate box

[ ]   [ ]   [ ]   [ ]   [ ]

Open-mindedness

| Shows bias towards certain individuals or cultures. | Accepts individual and cultural variations to an acceptable extent. Requires flexibility in approach. | Able to accept and respond appropriately to personal and cultural variations in behaviour. |

Tick appropriate box

[ ]   [ ]   [ ]   [ ]   [ ]

Sales ability

| Makes no attempt to demonstrate or discuss product or service features, or to establish customer requirements. | Offers product or service features, but needs more enthusiasm, conviction and care for customer needs. | Offers product or service features appropriate to customer needs with the aim of achieving customer satisfaction. |

Tick appropriate box

[ ]   [ ]   [ ]   [ ]   [ ]

CUSTOMER RELATIONS SKILLS

Patience

| Customer rushed through transaction. | Some extra care and attention shown. | Demonstrates extreme care, patience and tact, work permitting. |

Tick appropriate box

[ ]   [ ]   [ ]   [ ]   [ ]

Problem-solving

| Inconsistent approach. Unable to solve problem and deal with customer. Defensive. | Sound approach, but could improve on problem assessment and resolution. | Listens fully, uses analytical skills to resolve problem, communicates effectively and implements solutions. |

Tick appropriate box

[ ]   [ ]   [ ]   [ ]   [ ]

Customer needs analysis

| Misjudges needs. | Responds to customer requests giving full information or service. | Able to *anticipate* needs and provide service and information. |

Tick appropriate box

[ ]   [ ]   [ ]   [ ]   [ ]

Planning

| Haphazard approach. | Planning adequate, requiring attention to objective setting and realistic timing. | Uses behavioural, financial and other measurable objectives and deadlines for achievement of logically developed plans of action. |

Tick appropriate box

[ ]   [ ]   [ ]   [ ]   [ ]

COPING SKILLS

Problem-solving and decision-making

| Sound approach needing attention to creativity, consultation and commitment. | Unable to solve problems to the optimum satisfaction of all parties. | Fully assesses problems, uses creative and logical approach with consultation where necessary to solve problems and make decisions. In some cases is able to anticipate problems and act proactively. |

Tick appropriate box

[ ]   [ ]   [ ]   [ ]   [ ]

Assertiveness

| Unable to make a decision or judgement and state fully with reasons. Causes offence. | Mainly definite but occasionally gives way under pressure. | Uses assertive skills in a definite manner without causing offence. |

Tick appropriate box

[ ]   [ ]   [ ]   [ ]   [ ]

Stress management

| Cannot cope under pressure. | Performs adequately under time or situation constraints. | Develops priorities, retains calm approach and manages stress creatively. |

Tick appropriate box

[ ]   [ ]   [ ]   [ ]   [ ]

© 1994 Van der Wagen Consulting Pty Ltd.

|5

RECRUITMENT

SUMMARY

This chapter deals with the recruitment process. First, planning whether staff need to be full-time, part-time or casual, and second, deciding whether applications will be sought inside the organisation or if external recruitment is appropriate. The job descriptions and specifications described in the previous chapter will be used as the basis for recruitment efforts.

CHAPTER OBJECTIVES

On completion of this chapter you will be able to:

- establish a staffing need;
- evaluate recruitment sources;
- write advertisements;
- screen applicants on the telephone;
- conduct reference checks.

RECRUITMENT

Recruitment is the process of attracting suitable individuals to apply for employment with an organisation. This is more difficult than it would appear because if a very attractive position is advertised, and the minimum requirements are not sufficiently specific, the phones will ring for days and the office will be inundated with enquiries. If the advertisement is not clear about the position's requirements, a possible scenario is that an applicant might spend an hour trying to get through to apply, only to be told that the position needs someone with experience. This is immensely frustrating for people looking for work and many unfortunately give up because they become disheartened.

Of course, some companies face large numbers of employment enquiries without any advertising effort, simply because they have such a good image. The Hotel Inter-Continental in Sydney receives between twenty and fifty enquiries on an average day, and up to one hundred enquiries when they place an advertisement. (Incidentally, the hotel also receives up to forty enquiries a week from school leavers asking for work experience, this number peaking in February at up to one hundred calls and thirty letters daily!) The Commonwealth Bank receives an average of ninety application forms or unsolicited curriculum vitae and one hundred and twenty telephone enquiries per day. These figures increase by at least 50 per cent when advertisements are placed in the press.

'In my years as an interviewer I have talked to some of the most extraordinary people, ranging from the madly eccentric to the totally paranoid. One applicant followed me for days and threatened to jump off the Sydney Harbour Bridge if he was unsuccessful. Others arrived in transparent outfits, one in drag. One refused to tell me anything at all about herself. Despite the realisation that some applicants were clearly unsuitable, I always made the effort to interview them as best I could, and to consider everyone who applied as a sensitive person with the right to equal treatment, and to prompt replies to their application. If I was aware at the interview stage that they might be unsuccessful, I might say something like, "I have interviewed sixteen people for this position, some of whom are more experienced than you are, however your resume is very well presented and you have excellent results from college. I am sure you have a lot of potential for this industry. We will be developing a short list and will be in touch within four days." In this way they were not left with the impression that they stood a very good chance. Otherwise they might go home and wait, full of false expectations, for the phone to ring. Every Personnel Officer should be made to go out and apply for a job at least once a week. It doesn't take long to forget what it feels like to be at the other end. Job hunting would have to be one of life's most stressful experiences and careless treatment can destroy self-confidence.'

The aim of recruitment is to attract the best applicants and exclude any that are unsuitable. There is a fine line between the two: if one is too detailed in the specifications, not enough people will apply; and if one is too general, too many

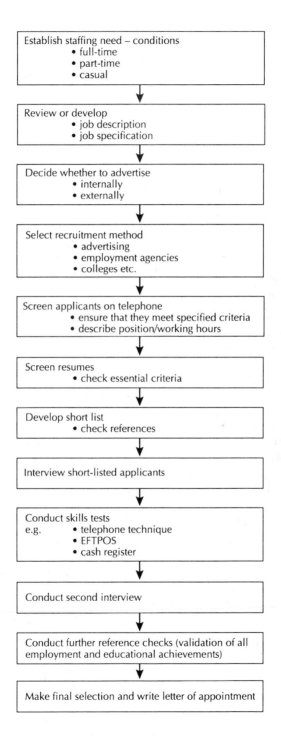

Figure 5.1   Recruitment and selection process

applicants to handle will make contact. Only experience and knowledge of the employment market is a guide in this.

ESTABLISH A STAFFING NEED
Full-time

Depending on award and enterprise agreements, full-time employment usually means working a forty-hour week. Hours in excess of eight hours per day generally attract overtime, and weekend work sometimes attracts additional payment (penalty rates). Many new employment arrangements are recognising the 24-hour nature of the service industry and reflect this in more flexible working arrangements. The benefits are that management is able to be more creative in rostering, and in doing so need not be too reliant on casual employees. For example, an arrangement to work between six and ten hours per day, averaged over a week, allows for better scheduling to meet customer needs during busy times and days of the week. From the employee point of view, full-time employment brings job security and better training and career development.

Part-time

Part-time employees work a limited number of hours per week, and enjoy the same benefits (holiday pay, sick leave etc.) as full-time staff. Managers generally find that part-time employees are excellent value for money: the arrangement suits both parties and results in low staff turnover. Changing lifestyles, family commitments and participation in sporting and other activities make this an attractive option for some people.

Casual

Casual employees work on an hourly basis. As they do not receive the same benefits (holiday pay, sick leave etc.) as part-time employees, their hourly rate is loaded accordingly. Generally speaking, casual employees do not have to be given notice. However, with increasing numbers of staff enjoying casual employment conditions, it is now becoming necessary to apply the same disciplinary principles as for other staff to avoid claims of unfair dismissal; see chapter thirteen for a discussion on this. While the employment of casual staff can solve short-term problems, there is a lack of commitment to the organisation's service ethic, and equally, a lack of commitment by the organisation to job security and career development.

At this point, following the establishment of a staffing need, the job description and job specification should be reviewed and updated. These describe the general tasks that form part of the job and the attributes, both procedural and personal, needed to provide quality service.

DECIDE WHETHER TO RECRUIT
INTERNALLY OR EXTERNALLY

Before any decision is made to recruit new staff, the experience and qualifications of current staff need to be considered as part of a 'promotion from within' policy. All vacancies should therefore be advertised on staff noticeboards before outside recruitment efforts commence. The benefits of internal recruitment are that morale is increased, induction is not necessary, the adjustment period is shorter and training usually progresses more rapidly. The greatest benefit of internal recruitment is that a far more accurate assessment of an individual's skills, knowledge and other attributes is possible. On the other hand, the benefits of external recruitment are the possible introduction of new ideas and insights into competitors.

The benefits of internal recruitment are thus:

- saves on cost of recruitment and selection;
- builds staff morale;
- reduces cost of induction and training;
- allows for succession planning;
- selection is based on actual performance assessment of current staff;
- provides career paths for employees.

The advantages of external recruitment are:

- brings in new skills and ideas;
- encourages competition;
- gives the organisation exposure in employment market;
- brings in applicants with current knowledge and qualifications.

Most organisations have a mix of internal and external recruitment, with external recruitment being considered only after the position has been advertised internally.

RECRUITMENT SOURCES

There are a number of sources for applicants other than newspapers, and one of the best is the educational and training institutions, most of which have employment notice boards. Depending on the seniority of the position, the following sources are suggested:

College and university noticeboards
Local area newspaper
City newspapers
National newspapers
Local noticeboards
Window or staff entry advertising
Trade magazines
Head hunting
Employment agencies

Staff recommendations
Employment services
Unsolicited applications and walk-ins

Advertising

The amount of detail included in the advertisement is usually determined by budget. However, this is often a false saving—a few extra words would not cost as much as the time taken to screen huge numbers of applicants, and managers should be mindful of this. 'Run-on advertisements', such as the one shown below, are the least expensive, followed by 'display advertisements' which can run from one column to four columns.

A run-on advertisement: A one-column display advertisement:

I need 5 part/full-time people to earn good money. No door to door selling. Call John NOW 888-8888

GOOD COMMUNICATOR?
* * * *
LOOKING FOR PART-TIME WORK?

We are seeking well-spoke community minded people to operate our new telemarketing centre. Excellent working conditions and pay. Previous experience not necessary.

Call Joan on 555-5555

Both of the above advertisements have obvious shortcomings; one can't imagine who would apply for the first without more details about how this money would be earned. Hopefully in the second, requiring 'well-spoke' people was a typing error. The less obvious shortcoming in both advertisements was that neither gave the address of the workplace.

Just as with the job description and job specification, the job advertisement should do two things: describe the duties involved, and specify the skills and experience necessary. The next four (display) advertisements achieve both ends; they explain the jobs and establish the requirements.

In designing an advertisement, the following points could be considered.

- Which items should be highlighted and where should they be placed? Should the company name and logo go at the top or the bottom? Should the position title feature at the top or in the middle?
- Is the text well set out and easy to read? (Point form is often useful here.)

Thomas Cook Inbound is an integral part of the global Thomas Cook travel service, providing high quality travel and accommodation for many Japanese tourists. We are seeking Japanese speaking, customer focused professionals who not only possess honorific Japanese skills and an understanding of Japanese culture, but who also wish to extend their skills. The following opportunities will be both challenging and highly satisfying.

Tour Guides

Responsible for leading tours, you will require at least 3 years travel industry experience, as well as strong public speaking, organisational and problem solving skills

Customer Service Co-ordinators

Positions available in Sydney/Cairns/Gold Coast and working a seven day roster. You will liaise directly with suppliers, Japanese speaking guides and guests on our popular tourist programmes, and as you will be organising reservation and travel documents, experience in the Japan inbound market is preferred. The ability to solve problems, meet deadlines and achieve results is equally important.

Excellent rewards and prospects await, so forward your resume, stating the position you are interested in to:

Mie Lim,
Inbound Division,
Thomas Cook Limited,
GPO Box 62, Sydney
NSW 2001.
Closing Date: 8 July 1994.

- Is the job described effectively? Is the advert positive and attractive?
- Are the requirements vague or specific?
- Is the form of reply stated clearly and is there a person nominated to answer enquiries?
- Is a closing date necessary for applications?
- Do you wish to limit calls to less busy times, such as between 9 and 11 a.m.?
- Is the suburb where the organisation is located given in the advertisement?

Written and produced by Beeley Callan Advertising

- Is the organisation portrayed in a positive light?
- How much will the advertisement cost, on which days will you place it, and in which section?

All advertising, and indeed the whole selection process, should comply with equal employment legislation.

SCREEN APPLICANTS ON THE TELEPHONE

Although asking applicants to submit their applications in writing is a feasible strategy, screening on the phone can save time for both parties. It gives the employer time to check that the applicant meets the minimum criteria specified in the advertisement (many people try their luck anyway) and to expand on the job requirements. Since advertising is so expensive, it also provides the opportunity to describe hours and days of work, routine duties etc. to callers.

SCREEN RESUMES

In screening submitted resumes, it is again necessary to establish whether the applicant has the necessary skills, experience, knowledge and other attributes required for the job. The first stage of screening can involve rejecting those unsuitable for these reasons. After this, the remaining applicants can be listed in order of preference.

DEVELOP SHORT LIST AND CHECK REFERENCES

At this point it is necessary to select candidates for interview and to advise those who have been unsuccessful (don't wait until the end of the whole selection process and make these people wait an unnecessarily long time for a response). It is also suggested that references are checked at this stage, unless they are submitted in writing. Most employers wait until after the interview to check references. However, as an interview takes at least half an hour and a reference check only a few minutes, this can save considerable time.

Employers providing information in response to reference checks should take care not to defame any applicant. The information provided should be documented (see chapter thirteen) and should be treated as confidential. Compton and Nankervis (1991, p. 208) point out that 'an employer may be able to claim qualified privilege under defamation laws, as long as the statement was not motivated by malice'.

The selection interview and the following four steps are part of the selection process, and will be discussed in detail in the next chapter. Brief descriptions of these steps are included here to give you the full sequence of recruitment.

INTERVIEW SHORT-LISTED CANDIDATES

All candidates should be asked the same questions, ones that have been carefully thought out beforehand and are based on the essential criteria for the job. Naturally this will lead to different follow-up questions, but each interview should follow a similar format in order to successfully differentiate between candidates.

REFERENCE CHECK FORM

JOB TITLE   *The position(s) held?*

_____

_____

DATES OF EMPLOYMENT   *Date of commencement and termination?*

_____

_____

DUTY SUMMARY   *Primary role?*

_____

_____

_____

SKILLS AND KNOWLEDGE   *Any particular skills or knowledge which may be relevant to future employment?*

_____

_____

_____

INTERPERSONAL RELATIONS   *Relations with internal customers—other departments, other staff and superiors?*

_____

_____

_____

CUSTOMER RELATIONS   *Relations with customers?*

_____

_____

_____

ACHIEVEMENTS AND PERFORMANCE ASSESSMENT *Any particular achievements such as promotion or outcomes of performance appraisal?*

_____

_____

_____

ABSENTEEISM OR WORKER'S COMPENSATION *History of absenteeism or Worker's Compensation claims?*

_____

_____

_____

CRITICAL INCIDENT *Would you please try to recall any incident that you can remember relating to providing service and describe the situation, including the role played by the employee?*

_____

_____

_____

_____

REASONS FOR LEAVING *Why did the employee leave?*

_____

_____

REHIRE? *Would you rehire without reservation?*

_____

_____

CONDUCT SKILLS TEST

At this stage a skills test can be conducted. This can be very short, but very productive. Examples include telephone answering, using EFTPOS machines and cash registers, selling merchandise or setting up restaurant tables.

SECOND INTERVIEWS

In larger organisations, second interviews are conducted with the immediate supervisor, who is then able to contribute to the final decision on which applicant should be offered the position.

CONDUCT FURTHER REFERENCE CHECKS AND VALIDATE INFORMATION ON THE APPLICATION FORM

If references have not already been checked, this is the appropriate time to do so. Where the position is a highly paid and extremely important one, all other details should be validated. A telephone call overseas can yield some most interesting information. This is illustrated by one employer's comments:

> 'We discovered only after he had joined us that the university course he had done was a one-day workshop. The way the resume was written it looked like a full-time course. Of course we had not checked overseas work references either. As it transpired, he hadn't been overseas at all.'

and another's:

> 'The importance of reference checking was brought home to me when I saw the saleslady who had been fired for stealing from the till working in the dress shop across the mall.'

MAKE FINAL SELECTION AND SEND LETTER OF APPOINTMENT

Having made the final selection, the successful applicant should be sent a letter of appointment, stating the position, specific working conditions and date of commencement.

EXERCISES AND DISCUSSION

1. Explain the differences between full-time, part-time and casual employment. List the advantages and disadvantages of employing staff with these conditions.

2. List the advantages and disadvantages of a 'promotion from within' policy (internal recruitment) and compare this with the advantages and disadvantages of an external recruitment policy.

3. Which source is likely to yield the highest number of applicants?

4. Are staff referrals a good source for recruitment?

5. How can poor recruitment practices breach equal employment legislation?

6. Do you think the name of the organisation or the title of the position should feature in large bold at the top of a display advertisement?

7. Read the following case study and discuss the approach taken by the manager and suggest how she might improve her recruitment practices. After reading the next chapter, you might like to return to this case study again and develop both recruitment and selection strategies for this retail outlet.

Case study—Joanna's retail outlet

Joanna is the store manager of a large retail outlet. She is short of staff and has advertised in the shop window. In fact, the store is nearly always short of staff and the notice in the window stays up permanently.

One Friday lunch time, a member of her staff brings an applicant to her. Joanna discovers that her name is Helen. She asks Helen to wait while she finishes a discussion with one of the staff over pricing. Finally, she starts to talk to Helen.

'Yes, sorry to keep you, we're always overworked on a Friday, and being short of staff doesn't help. But we all get on like a house on fire! What did you want to know about the job?'

'I wanted to know about the hours and the pay please, I've had some customer service experience and–' Helen is interrupted by one of the staff breaking in to speak to Joanna.

'Joanna, something has to be done about this, there is never enough change in the till and someone has to go to the bank now. Can you take over from me, or should I send someone else?'

'Sorry,' says Joanna. 'Helen, please hold on while I sort this out.'

Returning a few moments later, she asks Helen if she is married.

'Yes, I am,' Helen replies.

'Any kids?' Joanna asks.

'Yes, two, but my mother takes care of them,' Helen replies defensively.

'Sure, I was about to tell you about the hours. You need to be quite flexible.'

This time the phone rings and Joanna answers it. Midway through the call, she tells the person to hold on while she goes over to solve a problem with a customer in response to one of her staff gesturing for help.

Following this, Helen walks out.

6

SELECTION

SUMMARY

This chapter deals with the selection process, preparing interview questions, conducting the interview, evaluating applicants and writing a letter of appointment to the successful applicant.

CHAPTER OBJECTIVES

On completion of this chapter you will be able to:

- evaluate an application form in terms of position requirements and EEO guidelines;
- prepare appropriate and relevant interview questions;
- conduct an interview;
- complete an interview report form;
- write a letter of appointment.

SELECTION

In selecting staff, four outcomes are possible and these are shown in Figure 6.1, below. Obviously the aim of the selection process is to attract the highest calibre applicants to the organisation and select the best individual from these. With poor recruitment methods, too few applications are attracted (this is often inadvertently caused by the manager wanting to save time) and the 'best' people are left working for competitors. And selecting someone who turns out to be unsuitable is serious indeed. Dismissal is not an attractive prospect, and without extensive documentation this not easily done for minor performance problems. There are a number of costs associated with selecting and training staff, and having to resume the selection process is an expensive exercise. Added to costs such as advertising and interviewing is the cost of damage done to the organisation's service reputation by the employee's poor performance.

THE APPLICATION FORM

Having chosen a number of individuals to come in for an interview, the next step is to ask them to complete an application form, such as the one reproduced on pages

	APPLICANT SUITABLE	APPLICANT UNSUITABLE
EMPLOYED	Where this applicant is selected this is the ideal situation	Where this applicant is selected this spells disaster, huge financial and other cost to the organisation. Raises issues of dismissal and replacement.
REJECTED	Where is applicant is not selected through poor re-cruitment methods or lack of understanding of position requirements, this is a serious loss to the business since this is potentially the best applicant. Where applicant is rejected on grounds listed in anti-discrimi-nation legislation this could lead to court action.	Where unsuitable applicants are rejected for sound reasons this is appropriate.

Figure 6.1   Making the best selection decision

78–80. Often those who have provided extensive resumes ask why this is necessary. If this is the case, it is best to ask them to write a phrase such as 'Refer to my resume' in those sections of the application form that duplicate information. The main reasons for asking candidates to complete application forms are as follows.

- The form asks for very specific information, such as health issues, visa status and similar items which may not be covered in the resume, as it relates to the work performed.
- The applicant is asked to sign an agreement at the end of the form to verify the information included therein and to authorise the checking of background information. Deliberate errors can lead to dismissal and the applicant acknowledges this with their signature.
- The application form offers an opportunity to see the applicant's handwriting, which is sometimes relevant to the job.

With many resumes done professionally these days, it is easy to be misled by presentation, as was illustrated in the last chapter where inferences were made about the length of the university course. Here is another example of a selection process gone wrong:

'We employed an accountant who had lied about his age on the application form. We discovered this only on his first day when he joined the retirement fund and we had to let him go. He said he thought it would look better if he was older. If he thought his age might look better if he changed it, imagine what he might do to our records.'

The application form should be treated as confidential and the applicant's current employer should never be contacted without their consent.

CHOOSING INTERVIEW QUESTIONS

The interview questions should be chosen before the interview and should be based on the requirements listed in the job specification. In the job specification given the last chapter, the following criteria were selected as important for the position.

Experience

Has the person any experience in a similar or related capacity, or is familiar with any of the procedural aspects of the job (such as using a point-of-sale terminal)?

Education

Has the person received any appropriate formal training, or possesses any job-related knowledge that may be useful (such as handling credit card authorisations)?

Verbal communication

Verbal communication skills can be evaluated in the interview, with attention being paid to clarity, vocabulary, fluency etc.

APPLICATION FOR EMPLOYMENT

Position Applied For _____

Surname _____ Given Names _____

Preferred Form of Address (Mr, Mrs, Ms, Miss) _____

Address _____

_____

Postcode _____ Home Telephone Number (   ) _____

Date of Birth _____ Work Telephone Number (   ) _____

Are you an Australian Citizen or Permanent Resident?   Yes [   ]   No [   ]

If no, give type of visa _____

EDUCATIONAL QUALIFICATIONS

UNIVERSITY OR COLLEGE
(Start with your most recent or current study)

University/College _____ Date of Completion _____

Certificate _____

Subjects Attempted and Grades

_____

_____

University/College _____ Date of Completion _____

Certificate Awarded _____

SECONDARY

Name of High School _____

Certificate Awarded _____ Date of Completion _____

HSC Score (if applicable) _____

EMPLOYMENT HISTORY
(Start with your most recent or current job)

NAME AND ADDRESS OF EMPLOYER _____

_____

May we contact your current employer?   Yes [ ]   No [ ]   TEL (   ) _____

POSITION _____   FROM _____ TO _____

DUTIES AND RESPONSIBILITIES _____

_____

_____

NAME AND POSITION OF SUPERVISOR/MANAGER _____

REASON FOR LEAVING _____

NAME AND ADDRESS OF EMPLOYER _____

_____ TEL (   ) _____

POSITION _____   FROM _____ TO _____

DUTIES AND RESPONSIBILITIES _____

_____

_____

NAME AND POSITION OF SUPERVISOR/MANAGER _____

REASON FOR LEAVING _____

NAME AND ADDRESS OF EMPLOYER _____

_____ TEL (   ) _____

POSITION _____   FROM _____ TO _____

DUTIES AND RESPONSIBILITIES _____

_____

_____

NAME AND POSITION OF SUPERVISOR/MANAGER _____

REASON FOR LEAVING _____

NAME AND ADDRESS OF EMPLOYER _____

_____ TEL ( ) _____

POSITION _____ FROM _____ TO _____

DUTIES AND RESPONSIBILITIES _____

_____

_____

NAME AND POSITION OF SUPERVISOR/MANAGER _____

REASON FOR LEAVING _____

REFEREES

NAME _____ COMPANY _____

POSITION _____ TELEPHONE ( ) _____

NAME _____ COMPANY _____

POSITION _____ TELEPHONE ( ) _____

ANY FURTHER INFORMATION IN SUPPORT OF YOUR APPLICATION?

(Such as second language, other professional skills, equipment used or short courses completed)

_____

_____

_____

_____

_____

_____

_____

Non-verbal communication

Similarly, non-verbal communication skills can be evaluated in the interview, with attention paid to eye contact, facial expression, posture, gestures and voice qualities such as tone and pace.

Listening

The most important attribute of listening can also be assessed by watching for attentiveness and use of questions for clarification. The retention of information can be tested by asking the applicant a question about something that has been explained earlier.

Questions

The remaining attributes can be assessed using some questions that relate to the applicant's past experience. The phrasing of these questions to explore *past* experience is most important. To ask 'Do you get on with all types of people?' would be unproductive for two reasons. First, the answer would obviously be 'yes' (as a closed question was asked) and, second, people generally know what they *should* do; what they do or not is another story.

If you were to ask 'In your work situation in the past, what sorts of people have you found it hard to deal with?', the question might produce some quite revealing answers. Likewise, questions such as 'Thinking about your past experience, please describe a situation in which your patience was tested and explain what happened' will give a clearer insight into the person's skills in dealing with a range of people.

When phrasing interview questions, the aim is thus to explore past behaviour and to:

- not ask closed questions;
- not ask 'should' or 'would' questions; and
- not ask questions relating to marital status, racial origins, financial status, mode of transport, dependants, sports, hobbies and leisure activities, or any other aspects which are not directly relevant to the job.

For the skills listed in the earlier job specification the following questions have been developed.

Showing initiative

In your past experience have there been situations in which you have been able to make suggestions about improvements? Can you explain how you approached the issue?

Establishing customer needs

In your previous dealings with customers, can you think of one for whom it was an important decision and explain how you went about making the sale.

Flexibility

Thinking about your recent experience with customers, can you describe and contrast two customers whose expectations were different and explain how you dealt with them?

Problem-solving

We all face difficult situations in customer service. Can you think of one such situation which was a real challenge to your problem-solving skills and explain how you handled it?

Time management

Typically, customers arrive all at once and it is difficult to cope under pressure. Can you explain how you have coped in the past when faced with more customers than usual?

These are just some ideas for the type of questions that could be prepared beforehand. Remember, the criteria for selection should be directly related to performance on the job. A most interesting newspaper article has been reproduced here. Would body odour be a relevant criterion when selecting someone to sell perfume? Is this factor relevant to her employment? The judge thought so, and was thus grounds for dismissal.

Saleswoman too smelly to sell perfume, judge rules

TORONTO, Tuesday: A judge upheld the sacking of a Calvin Klein fragrance demonstrator who was dismissed by her employer because the company believed her body odour made her a poor perfume saleswoman.

Ms Sharon Bagnall was sacked by Calvin Klein Canada in 1991 for what the company termed a "serious personal hygiene problem" and for alleged disruptive behaviour at odds with the cosmetic giant's image.

Ms Bagnall, 52, fought back with a $US150,000 ($A206,000) law suit alleging that she was wrongfully dismissed. Witnesses said at her trial that she was always impeccably groomed, did not smell and acted professionally on the job.

But in a decision released yesterday, Justice Lee Ferrier, of Ontario Court's general division, said he believed the Calvin Klein witnesses, who said Ms Bagnall smelt like an armpit.

Ms Bagnall said of the decision: "I'm stunned. I felt like I died all over again. I only did this for justice, not money, and I only told the truth.

"I don't have a job, I haven't had work for a long time and I don't have a bank account. I don't have anything."

Justice Ferrier awarded Ms Bagnall $US5,028 in additional severance pay but denied any other claims against Calvin Klein, saying the company gave her several chances to clean up her act and did not sack her to be mean.

"It is my finding that, on occasion, [Bagnall's] clothing had a stale odour of underarm perspiration," Justice Ferrier wrote in his ruling.

"It was by no means a daily occurrence, but it did occur ..."

Ms Bagnall had worked as a fragrance demonstrator for 18 months at Calvin Klein counters in Toronto department stores before she was sacked.

Associated Press

(© 1994 AAP Information
Services Pty Ltd)

ANTI-DISCRIMINATION AND EEO

Anti-discrimination legislation makes it unlawful to discriminate on the basis of race, colour, sex, sexual preference, age, physical or mental disability, marital status, family responsibilities, pregnancy, religion, political opinion, national extraction or social origin.

Equal Employment Opportunity (EEO) is the opportunity for all individuals to be employed and progress in employment of the basis of merit.

These general principles need to be borne in mind in the selection process, and later in training and development.

THE INTERVIEW

Generally, the interview starts with some general conversation to put the applicant at ease. If the interviewer is going to use the behavioural style of interview suggested above, it might be an idea to give a copy of the questions to the applicant a few minutes beforehand. With this degree of difficulty in the phrasing of the questions (it takes time to think up examples), this strategy gives the person time to prepare. Alternatively, the questioning phase of the interview needs to be preceded with an explanation of the type of question and a reassurance that time can be taken before answering.

It is useful to organise the interview into four stages:

Stage I—Introduction
Stage II—Questioning
Stage III—Explanation
Stage IV—Conclusion.

Following the introduction, the questioning can begin with the assurance that as much time as necessary is available to answer. It is always a good idea to start off with some simple questions, perhaps confirming some of the details in the application form to encourage the applicant and allow their confidence to build. The aim should be to enable the interviewee to present him or herself in the best light, so that they can leave feeling positive about the interview and their performance. Some applicants need more prompting than others, and follow-up questions can be used in all cases to encourage more detailed answers. The interview should not put them under undue pressure or leave them feeling disheartened. A recent applicant for the position of doorman at a city five-star hotel reported that he had been asked seventy questions in the first interview!

After most questioning is completed, the job can be described in detail, including working conditions and other relevant information.

Some interviewers prefer to have the explanation before the questioning, but there are two advantages in having it afterwards. The first is that the applicant is far more likely to listen attentively after the questioning is completed. If lengthy explanations start the interview, the applicant is so keyed up that very little information is absorbed. Rapport can be built up during the questioning period and following this, the applicant can relax and listen to the description of the job and working conditions. The second reason for having the explanation as stage III is that if the applicant is clearly suitable for the position, it allows the interviewer to go into more detail, and then possibly ask a few more in-depth questions. In the final stages of the interview, the interviewer needs also to test for listening by asking a question that relates to something the applicant has been told earlier. This is also an opportunity to ask whether there is anything further the applicant would like to add in support of their application and also to ask whether there are any questions they would like answered.

The last stage of the interview is the conclusion, where the applicant should be advised of the time that will be taken to reach a decision and the date when they can expect a reply. This is a good opportunity to advise them that they were selected from a large group of applicants (mention the number to give them some encouragement) and to give a general idea, where possible, of the calibre of other applicants. One needs to be careful here not to infringe EEO guidelines and to select only on the basis of criteria which are directly and substantially relevant to the position vacant.

Listening during the interview

Efforts to phrase good questions are quite wasted if the interviewer does not listen carefully or does not allow the applicant to speak. The interviewer should never dominate the interview and should not spend inordinate amounts of time on lengthy explanations. In balance, the applicant should spend at least 60 per cent of the interview talking.

There are several ways in which listening can be enhanced:

- letting the applicant expand on answers in response to non-verbal encouragement;
- giving them full attention;
- avoiding all noise or disturbance;
- allowing pauses and silences to allow the applicant time to gather their thoughts;
- repeating part of an answer to confirm that you are listening carefully;
- listening for meaning, and asking questions for clarification.

Taking notes

Although note-taking is difficult in the interview, it is essential to make some notes afterwards. This can be done using a criterion-referenced chart such as the one shown here. Although claims of discrimination are unlikely if selection is based on job-related criteria, it is still useful to have notes as the basis for the decision-making process. These can also be useful if looking for another staff member at a later date, especially as this avoids advertising and starting the selection process again.

Essentially, selecting staff is a process of discriminating. However, it is discriminating on criteria which are relevant and defensible. By using the

INTERVIEW REPORT FORM

NAME OF APPLICANT   Date of interview: _____

_____

POSITION

_____

DEPARTMENT

_____

EXPERIENCE

_____

_____

[ ]	[ ]	[ ]	[ ]
None	Not relevant	Relevant	Directly relevant

EDUCATION AND TRAINING

_____

_____

[ ]	[ ]	[ ]	[ ]
None	Not relevant	Relevant	Directly relevant

JOB CONTENT KNOWLEDGE   *Demonstrates knowledge of procedures, methods and requirements and applies these in the performance of tasks.*

_____

_____

[ ]	[ ]	[ ]	[ ]
Does not meet requirements	Meets requirements	Above requirements	Exceeds requirements

VERBAL COMMUNICATION SKILLS   *Speaks clearly and audibly, using appropriate vocabulary.*

_____

_____

[ ]	[ ]	[ ]	[ ]
Does not meet requirements	Meets requirements	Above requirements	Exceeds requirements

NON-VERBAL COMMUNICATION SKILLS   *Reinforces verbal messages through use of gestures and facial expression. Demonstrates confidence and enthusiasm in voice qualities and posture.*

[ ]	[ ]	[ ]	[ ]
Does not meet requirements	Meets requirements	Above requirements	Exceeds requirements

LISTENING   *Listens attentively, asks relevant questions and recalls information.*

[ ]	[ ]	[ ]	[ ]
Does not meet requirements	Meets requirements	Above requirements	Exceeds requirements

ABILITY TO ESTABLISH CUSTOMER NEEDS   *Uses questioning skills and non-verbal cues to evaluate customer needs to clearly describe only relevant product features or benefits.*

[ ]	[ ]	[ ]	[ ]
Does not meet requirements	Meets requirements	Above requirements	Exceeds requirements

ABILITY TO SHOW INITIATIVE   *Intervenes where appropriate, offers assistance where necessary. Makes suggestions, offers information and service.*

[ ]	[ ]	[ ]	[ ]
Does not meet requirements	Meets requirements	Above requirements	Exceeds requirements

SALES ABILITY   *Assists customer with decision-making and closes sale.*

[ ]	[ ]	[ ]	[ ]
Does not meet requirements	Meets requirements	Above requirements	Exceeds requirements

FLEXIBILITY   *Responds appropriately to interpersonal and intercultural differences.*

_____

_____

[ ]   [ ]   [ ]   [ ]
Does not meet   Meets   Above   Exceeds
requirements   requirements   requirements   requirements

PROBLEM-SOLVING   *Identifies problems, obtains and evaluates facts, generates solutions, implements and follows up on results.*

_____

_____

[ ]   [ ]   [ ]   [ ]
Does not meet   Meets   Above   Exceeds
requirements   requirements   requirements   requirements

TIME MANAGEMENT   *Sets priorities and copes calmly with pressure.*

_____

_____

[ ]   [ ]   [ ]   [ ]
Does not meet   Meets   Above   Exceeds
requirements   requirements   requirements   requirements

SUMMARY OF REFEREE'S REPORT

_____

_____

_____

DECISION

_____

_____

WHAT THE APPLICANT WAS TOLD

_____

_____

LETTER OF APPOINTMENT

Dear [Name],

We are pleased to welcome you as an employee of [name of business]. We hope that we will be able to meet your expectations of your new position and that we will be able to assist you in achieving your long-term career plans.

As discussed in your interview, you will be employed as a [full-time/part-time/casual] employee as a [classification] to commence work on [date of commencement].

The following conditions of employment apply,
[elaborate on terms and conditions].

Our organisation takes pride in its ability to meet customer needs, and quality service is our aim. We hope to do everything possible to assist you in doing so, by providing systems and procedures, and by training you in areas in which you would like to enhance your skills. At times you will be directed to perform certain duties and you are expected to follow these instructions and to work competently for the sake of both customers and other employees. In response to our customer's needs there may be changes to your duties or your hours of work in the future, and we expect that you will be able to alter hours and perform a range of tasks as required.

You will be provided with an employee handbook and will also have all rules, regulations and policies explained to you. It is your responsibility to ensure that you are aware of all company policies, that you keep up to date by reading information circulated and that you attend meetings when necessary.

In selecting and training staff to deliver quality service, we hope to achieve both customer and employee satisfaction. If at any time you do not feel that we are achieving these aims please discuss these issues with your supervisor.

Welcome again to [business name]. We are looking forward to seeing you on your first day. Please report to [name] at [location].

Please indicate your acceptance of the position offered by signing and returning one copy of this letter.

[Signed]
Manager/Human Resource Manager

behavioural interviewing approach (Green 1982), in which past behaviour is used to predict future behaviour, a better decision is possible. Its aim is to find evidence relating to the applicant's attributes. For this reason, all questioning should be directed to the past and not towards what the person may do, or thinks they should do, in the future.

LETTERS OF APPOINTMENT

When the final decision has been made and the person has accepted the position, a letter of appointment (such as the sample one given here) should be sent to confirm the details. This letter should state:

- the position
- a summary of the position's duties
- the department or location of the position
- the reporting relationship
- the position's grade
- the pay rate, and
- conditions of employment.

This contractual arrangement is important from an industrial relations point of view. The following two examples illustrate why this letter of appointment needs to be very specific. First, a chef was employed and paid a rate far in excess of the labour agreement for chefs in the industry, on the basis that overtime would not be paid. However, after some years the chef decided to claim his overtime on the higher rate of pay. There was no written agreement on record to show the previous informal arrangement. Second, an insurance salesman, who for years had worked on commission, claimed that he was an employee of the company and was entitled to long service leave. Again the employment relationship was unclear.

EXERCISES AND DISCUSSION

1. First impressions are very important. The interview is the first impression the applicant has of the organisation. How might these impressions be influenced?

2. Why is it useful to have the applicant complete an application form?

3. For the job description you wrote on completion of chapter four for a bank teller or waiter, develop some interview questions and a form to evaluate interview performance.

4. The following were once listed as key interview subjects for interviews. Which do you think are appropriate and which not?

Bibliographical detail
Do they live close to work? What are their physical capabilities? Are they the right age and do they have dependants?

Motivation
Do they have a desire to work, and a supportive family? Are their expectations realistic? Do they need the income, or have financial commitments?

5. Explain the stages of an interview and justify your thinking.

6. Write a letter of appointment for the person in question 3.

|7

INDUCTION

SUMMARY

This chapter covers the topic of induction, the process of ensuring that new employees become capable and confident in the shortest possible time. It also ensures that they are fully aware of their obligations and of the organisation's service philosophy.

CHAPTER OBJECTIVES

On completion of this chapter you will be able to:

- explain the purpose of employee induction;
- develop an induction checklist;
- plan a formal orientation session;
- describe the benefits of successful induction to the new employee;
- describe the benefits of successful induction to the organisation.

INDUCTION

Induction is the process of assimilating new employees into the organisation as smoothly and effectively as possible. The main aim of this process is to socialise employees, to make them familiar with their new environment, to introduce them to other employees and to enable them to offer quality service with a solid foundation of product and procedural knowledge in the shortest possible time. The induction should cover information relating to daily work routines, information relating the organisation's history, aims and service philosophy, and information relating to organisational rules and policies.

The checklist opposite is a useful tool in the induction process as it ensures that all aspects are covered in detail. With such an enormous amount of important information, clearly not all of it should be discussed at one time. The employee's first day should be a settling-in period; information overload is definitely not appropriate! Many new employees report going home feeling shell-shocked after their first day in a new job. These early experiences can have a profound effect on future perceptions, and for this reason the manager should ensure that, at the end of the first day, the new employee is familiar with the work environment, has met immediate colleagues and has only been given limited information.

Over the following few days and weeks, other information can be supplied. This is sometimes done as a formal orientation session attended by senior management, where the company history, goals and strategic plans are explained to new staff. At the same time, security, health and safety issues can be covered by a member of the Security Department, payroll issues by a member of the Payroll Department, and customer service issues by Sales and Marketing or the Training Manager. At this point, many service organisations give new staff a complete tour of the organisation and, if possible, a taste of what it is like to be a customer. In the hospitality industry, staff should have the opportunity to dine in restaurants. This is a fitting conclusion to an orientation session. In large retail organisations, new staff could be sent in as mystery customers and asked to report on the service they experienced. Staff in the banking industry could be asked to open new accounts. Developing an awareness of the customer's viewpoint is an essential component of any induction or training program focused on customer service.

The induction checklist shown is therefore intended to cover several days and weeks. It is important that none of these details are neglected and that the employee signs an acknowledgment that they have been fully informed of their rights and obligations. The manager is primarily responsible for the induction process, but the Human Resources Department plays an important role in providing the employee handbook and running formal orientation sessions. In smaller operations, the manager or supervisor is responsible for all aspects of the induction process.

INDUCTION CHECKLIST

ARRIVAL

Tour of department area
Lockers and toilets
Staff canteen/meals
Parking

INTRODUCTIONS

Supervisor
Manager
Colleagues

TERMS OF ENGAGEMENT

Job description
Contract of employment
Classification (grade)
Shift work
Probation
Notice

ATTENDANCE

Reporting of absence
Working hours
Time recording
Leaving work area
Meal and other breaks
Annual leave
Long service and maternity leave

PAY AND DEDUCTIONS

Method and time of payment
Deductions including tax
Union Membership
Superannuation
Overtime and other entitlements

SAFETY

Fire and evacuation
Reporting of accidents

Occupational Health and Safety
  Regulations
Safety Committee
Protective clothing
Equipment
Safety procedures and training
Worker's Compensation claims
First aid

RULES, REGULATIONS AND POLICIES

Equal Employment Opportunity
Promotion from within
Sexual Harassment
Affirmative Action
Uniforms
Telephone calls
Ethical conduct
Confidentiality
Dismissal policy (with warnings)
Summary dismissal (grounds for)
Loss prevention, control systems

CAREER DEVELOPMENT

Training and assessment of
  competency-based modules
Career progression
Transfer and promotion
Educational assistance
Counselling

ORIENTATION SESSION

Introduction to Heads of Departments
Company mission/aims/objectives
Organisation structure/chart
Sales marketing
The customers
Quality standards
Tour of organisation
Being a customer

AIMS OF INDUCTION

- That the employee is made to feel welcome and feel part of a cohesive group as rapidly as possible.
- That the employee is able to identify with organisational goals, including quality of service.
- That the employee is familiar with requirements of regular or VIP customers, and with all other primary market segments and their identified needs.
- That the employee is able to see that his or her own needs for training, development and progression will be met.
- That employee is advised of relevant and important information at a rate which he or she can handle (not all on the first day), such as those listed on the checklist.
- That all important information is given in writing, preferably in the form of an employee handbook.
- That the employee acknowledges receipt of the above information and signs the checklist to confirm this.
- That the employee's comprehension of vital information is tested, such as fire and emergency procedures.
- That the employee is able to recognise senior management, and is shown around areas other that the immediate workplace.
- That the employee has a copy of the relevant job description.
- That the employee is clear about lines of communication, responsibilities and relevant limits of authority.
- That the employee is aware of relevant legislation such as Trade Practices, Liquor Licensing and Food Acts, which may have a bearing on the organisation and its operation.
- That the employee is aware of programs such as Health and Safety, Affirmative Action, Sexual Harassment etc.
- That the employee knows where to get help if it is needed.
- That the employee is aware of the importance of their role in the organisation.

THE EMPLOYEE HANDBOOK

The employee handbook is a valuable source of information for all employees, most particularly those who have just commenced with the organisation. It should provide details of the topics listed earlier in the induction checklist, such as attendance, safety, rules and policies. A copy of the handbook should be sent out with the letter of appointment, allowing the employee to start to understand something of the company mission, communication strategies, customer focus and other related issues that will be discussed in the first days of employment, as well as in the formal orientation process.

The handbook is a most important reference for all employees who need to review policies at times most relevant to them. As a preventative measure in claims of unfair dismissal, it also spells out company rules in detail so that mis-

SAMPLE ORIENTATION SESSION

8.30 a.m.	Tea and coffee served
8.45	Introduction by the Training Officer
9.00	Address by the General Manager
9.15	Company history, mission and objectives (slides and video where possible)
9.45	Introduction to other senior staff
10.00	Coffee break, followed by a tour of premises
11.30	Safety, security and health issues
12.30 p.m.	Lunch
1.30	Communication
	Internal and external
	Meetings
	Newsletters
	Memos
	Suggestion programs
	Customer focus groups
2.00	Customers
	Internal and external
	Seeking customer feedback
	Value of customer feedback
	Anticipating needs
	Ideas and solutions
	Team efforts
	Incentive programs
2.45	Video—*Customer focus group: closing the feedback loop*
3.00	Coffee break
3.15	Training and career development
	In-house and external training
	Competency-based training
	Recognition of prior learning
	Performance appraisal
	Career progression
	Pay and incentives
4.00	Company mission (what we want to achieve) and ethics (how we would like to achieve it)
4.15	Being the customer—your opportunity
4.45	Discussion and close

understandings do not occur. The handbook should also describe the performance appraisal or competency-based training system and the development of skills and knowledge to enhance the employee's skills and achievement. The delivery of quality service, and what this entails for the organisation and the individual is clearly one of the topics that should be covered in the handbook. This philosophy will be reinforced at different times in the person's career, but the importance of early first impressions cannot be underestimated. Early understanding of the organisation's commitment to its customers, and equally to its staff, will set the tone for a positive working climate.

BENEFITS OF SUCCESSFUL SOCIALISATION

The benefits of formal and informal induction processes are many. From the employer's point of view, these are:

- the employee becomes productive quickly;
- the employee adopts the organisation's service philosophy;
- the employee is committed to organisational goals and objectives;
- early expectations influence stability in the short and long-term, increasing commitment and reducing staff turnover.

From the employee's point of view the advantages are:

- anxiety is reduced;
- integration with team members is achieved;
- employer expectations are clear;
- performance standards are spelt out;
- a sense of belonging emerges.

REVIEW PERIODS

The information given to new employees should be reviewed and updated on a continuous basis. A review after the first week and the first month are appropriate to reinforce the key points and to ensure that the employee has settled in and is confident in their new role. Following this, there should be ongoing efforts to update employees on changes to strategic planning, their conditions of employment, marketing efforts and so on. This sense of belonging can only occur when employees feel themselves to be an integral and important part of the organisation. This can be encouraged through the use of company newsletters, departmental meetings and the like.

Unfortunately, for many employees the orientation session is the only time that they see senior members of staff in their entire working lives. This is particularly the case for very junior employees, some of whom have daily contact with customers, and for whom the induction session (when the service philosophy was explained) is a hazy memory. Large-scale formal meetings of staff and senior management on an annual basis need to be considered so that relevant information is communicated to all employees in something other than written form. The use of slides, video, short training exercises and, most importantly, customer feedback (bring in some real live ones!) can enhance this presentation and further contribute to an ongoing sense of commitment and belonging.

EXERCISES AND DISCUSSION

1. Your employees are handling large amounts of money and have access to confidential information. Write a section for an employee handbook on these issues (you may like to refer to the employee's common law obligations to account to the employer for all monies and properties received in the course of employment, and to be faithful to the employer's interests).

2. If you looked at the induction process from an employee's point of view, what would your priorities be for your first days and weeks?

3. Looking at induction from a management viewpoint, prioritise the information you would like to pass on to your new employees.

4. Which aspects of employee induction do you think should be done formally, with a group of new staff, and which do you think should be done informally, on an individual basis?

5. How would you run an employee information session for staff who have been with the company for some time and need to be updated? Would you invite them to join an orientation session for new staff?

8

STAFF TRAINING:
one-to-one instruction
(procedural dimension
of service)

SUMMARY

This chapter deals with training from the traditional viewpoint, with the four-step process (planning, demonstrating, practice and review) the method used to teach new staff how to follow operational guidelines (procedures). As such, it covers writing learning outcomes, planning for training, presenting the program, organising application of the information, giving feedback, and evaluating the success of the training program.

CHAPTER OBJECTIVES

On completion of this chapter you will be able to:

- conduct a training needs analysis;
- write learning outcomes;
- plan training sessions;
- present training material in a way which is effective for the trainee;
- supervise practice;
- give performance feedback.

STAFF TRAINING

Quality initiatives, such as Quality Management (the ISO 9000 or local equivalents) usually entail development and implementation of standard procedures and review processes. These review processes are most important in a changing world where procedures need to be adapted in response to the internal and environmental factors influencing the operation of the organisation. At the start of any quality initiative there is, however, the development of standard operational procedures based on strategic planning and cost analysis. Insofar as employee performance is concerned, these procedures should take into account job design factors to ensure that staff are multiskilled, that their work is challenging, that they have a degree of autonomy and that performance feedback is based on quantitative and qualitative measures.

Given that these procedures have been established, responsive as they should be to changing circumstances, the next step is training staff in the implementation of these procedures to meet predefined standards of performance. These performance standards qualify and quantify performance outcomes. In simple terms, the procedure defines the steps to be followed in the performance of a task, where

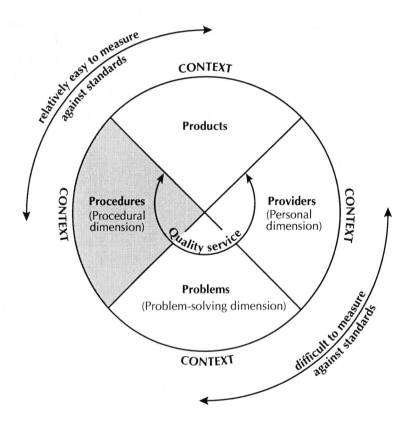

Figure 8.1 Training for the procedural dimension of service

DON'T sneeze in the bank ... The treasurer of the Apex Club of Tuggeranong, getting ready for the auditor, realised he didn't have six pages of statements from various Westpac accounts. Could he have reprints? Yes, at $7 a sheet, total $42. Some pages, when received, had no transactions on them. Oh yes, said the bank, the original wouldn't have been sent because there were no transactions. Still pay that $42.

(SMH, 12/6/94)

the performance standards define how success is measured. Performance standards are quite obvious to many supervisors and managers. Differences in perception as to what is 'good enough' often result in conflict between staff and management, with the attitude of many staff being that 'near enough is good enough'. This is not a deliberate philosophy based on laziness, but is often attributable to ignorance of the standards required, and the reasons why the standards are so important to the success of the operation.

Employees working at the luxury end of the service sector are often staggered by the expectations of their superiors and clients. If their idea of an expensive holiday is a trip into the country by car, a world cruise is beyond their imagining. If the most they would ever spend on a precious stone is a month's pay, developing rapport with a wealthy customer may be somewhat difficult. If their bathroom at home hasn't been cleaned for a month, much less spring-cleaned in a year, then a Housekeeper's expectation that a hotel bathroom is so clean that no sign of previous use is evident (in even the deepest recesses) may appear unrealistic and unnecessary. The importance of implementing high quality standards is a crucial issue in training staff. In all stages of training, the employee needs to know why things are done in a certain way, and what the consequences would be if standards are not met.

'The customers were livid. They expected a beach holiday at a resort, and you sent them to Suva!'

'I thought all the hotels in Fiji were on the beach.'

'Well, why didn't you ask? Or look it up? You just invented it all the details as you went along. Aqua-sailing, para-gliding, water skiing, I ask you! There are brochures, you know!'

'I didn't realise that it wasn't what they wanted. They should have been clearer.'

'We're not selling cheese sandwiches! You have to find out exactly what your customer wants. You have to question, question, question, and then confirm, confirm, confirm. For them, this is a really important decision. You'll never make it with your attitude. Everything on the booking advice was wrong. You miscalculated the time differences, they missed connecting flights, even the day was wrong!'

Training staff to follow procedures entails planning the training outcomes and content, preparing carefully for the training presentation and presenting the steps in an effective manner. Following this, the last and most important step is giving the employee the opportunity to practise what they have been taught, until they are confident and the trainer is convinced that the training objectives have been reached.

However, before training can begin, a training needs analysis is necessary to determine the training need. This may sound obvious but it is not uncommon in industry for training to be seen as a solution to non-training problem. Staff may not be following company procedures for a number of motivational or other reasons and it is valuable to ensure that a training problem exists before commencing the development and implementation of a new one.

CONDUCTING A TRAINING NEEDS ANALYSIS

The first step in a training needs analysis (Figure 8.2) is to describe the performance required, in this case, the procedures that need to be followed to perform a task in a satisfactory manner. This can be done by reviewing the job description (which

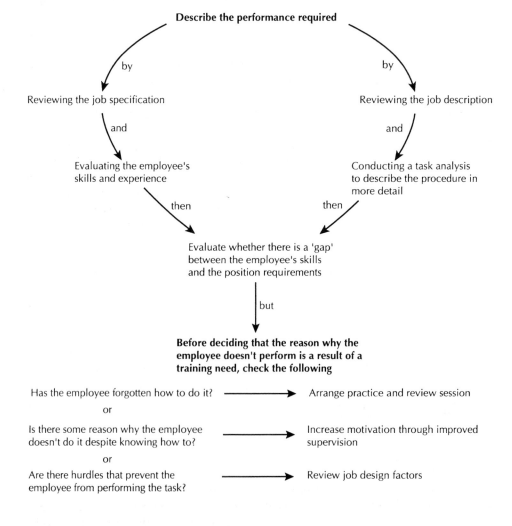

Figure 8.2 Training needs analysis

describes the duties performed in the job) and by conducting a task analysis to break down these procedures into steps. At the same time, it is useful to review the job specification (which describes the skills and experience required to fill the position) and to evaluate the employee in these terms. Staff shortages often lead to the rapid selection and employment of individuals who have skill deficiencies; these deficiencies will become more obvious in this process.

Finally, by comparing the employee's skills with the tasks that need to be performed in following company procedures, the trainer can evaluate whether there is a 'gap' between the employee's skills and the position requirements.

This is not the end of the story. Failure to follow procedures is often attributable to a range of other reasons, such as laziness, lack of practise or shortage of supplies. Therefore, before concluding that a training need exists, the trainer should also ask some of the following questions.

Has the employee forgotten how to do it?

If the employee has forgotten how to a procedure is performed, then a review session and some practice are all that is needed to remedy the situation.

Is there some reason why the employee doesn't do it, despite knowing how to?

Getting away with short cuts is a strong reason not to perform to standard, as it allows the employee more time on other things such as talking and daydreaming. The fact that non-performance has not been noticed or mentioned is an incentive to continue in the same manner. If the procedures are to be adhered to correctly, encouragement is needed to ensure that compliance occurs. The remedy in this case is increased motivation through more effective supervision.

Not following safety procedures, forgetting to report maintenance problems and ignoring customer complaints are examples of common performance problems. An explanation of the reasons why these are important and the serious risks involved may be all that is required to increase motivation. In this case the risks are to the employee's health, the company's success, and the future employment of all personnel.

Are there hurdles that prevent the employee from performing the task?

Peer pressure can lead to low levels of performance, as can shortages of supplies and a lack of co-operation from other departments and staff members. These possibilities need to be considered in detail before a training solution is proposed to solve a performance problem.

PLANNING

The first step in preparing a training session is to decide what is to be taught in terms of 'learning outcomes'. By deciding in advance the outcomes desired, the trainer has a very clear idea of what needs to be achieved by the employee. This is important for both their sakes. It is highly rewarding for an employee (trainee) to achieve a goal that has been spelt out before the training commences. It gives a sense of direction and motivation. The other reason is the sense of achievement for the trainer when he or she sees that learning has occurred and that they too have been successful in training correctly.

Learning outcomes are also known as training objectives. Whatever they are called, all have three parts: the definition of the task to be performed; the standard required; and the conditions or circumstances under which the task is to be performed.

THE TASK AND CONDITIONS OR CIRCUMSTANCES AND STANDARD TO BE REACHED.

An example of a learning outcome for someone taking an order could be:

'On completion of training, the trainee will be able to take an order that is accurate, legible and complete, using a standard order form.'

If a computer system were used, this would change the learning outcome to:

'On completion of training, the trainee will be able to take a reservation, using RPD software, that is efficient, accurate and complete.'

The performance standards are most important as they define 'what good looks like'. In example above, speedy keyboard entry will ensure efficiency, a lack of errors will ensure accuracy, and careful entries in all reservations fields will ensure completeness. These measures of success are most important in the training process. It is essential that the trainee knows the criteria by which the performance will be judged. This leads then to intrinsic motivation as the goal is achieved.

In service industries, routine procedures lend themselves well to this type of training. A task analysis will yield the steps involved in following procedures such as taking reservations, cancelling bookings, handling requests for credit, opening accounts and processing payments.

Having planned the learning outcomes, the next step is to create a lesson plan that carefully details the steps to be followed in the demonstration, the facts or knowledge to be taught while demonstrating, and the questions that will be asked. The content of the presentation also needs to be planned to meet the needs of the trainee, and any language difficulty or other factor needs to be considered here as well. An important part of this planning process is also deciding upon equipment and other aids that may be necessary.

In conclusion, the planning process needs to cover the following questions:

Who—Who is to be taught, what are their special needs, and how much do they know already?

What—What is to be taught, and how can this be broken down into steps?

Why—Why is it important that this procedure is followed in the way it is being taught?

How—How will the demonstration be conducted and the information necessary be communicated?

When—When will the training occur and how long will it take?

Exercises

1. If you were teaching someone to cross the road in the country, what would you plan as a learning outcome for your trainee?
2. Asking someone to make you a cup of tea is not uncommon. How would you decide whether the cup of tea had met your standards? What if you had not spelt out your requirements beforehand?
3. If you were training someone in dental hygiene, what learning outcome would you expect from your trainee?

These are all everyday procedures. Remember that you have been asked about learning outcomes. These are goals, the final results of your training—the way in which success will be measured. They are *not the procedures* themselves; those will be spelt out later.

Answers

1. On completion of training, the trainee will be able to cross a double lane, quiet country road without endangering their own or anyone else's safety.
   (Note that this will be achieved by following the correct procedure, but this is not yet spelt out, as this is the outcome of the training only. Visions of this trainee getting safely to the other side, but causing an accident in doing so, prompted the inclusion of 'anyone else's' safety as a performance standard.)
2. The performance standard for my cup of tea is weak with two sugars. How about you? If we can't agree on performance standards for such a simple thing, imagine our different expectations in whole range of other tasks!
3. Upon completion of training, the trainee should be able to clean their teeth (performance/task) using a toothbrush and paste (conditions) so that all visible plaque is removed from the teeth (modest performance standard).

PRESENTATION

Introduction to the training

The lesson should have some specific points covered at the start. These are important for the trainee. They include an explanation of the learning outcomes to be achieved and the associated standards. As mentioned earlier, intrinsic satisfaction occurs when the trainee sees that their efforts are achieving the desired outcome. This form of goal setting is a feature that is often neglected in training, the goals of training being obvious to the trainer (although many a trainer has delivered training without any clear idea of the objectives). It assists the trainee at other times when the trainer is not present to encourage or correct. Being able to apply standards to performance is a key attribute desired in staff who continually learn from their experience.

Next, the trainee needs to be told why the procedures or tasks are important. Without an explanation of the possible consequences of not using safety equipment, or confirming credit card numbers or confirming dates and times, the trainee is not motivated to follow the instructions to the letter. The more powerful reasons given for compliance to company procedures and their attendant standards, the more likely that the employee listens, applies him or herself to the task or transfers the learning to the workplace. In the sample lesson plan given later in this chapter, the trainee is given several reasons for careful and correct application of adhesive dressings. This simple task is likely to be neglected unless they are aware of the possible outcomes of severe infections or acquisition of blood-borne pathogens, such as AIDS and hepatitis, through open wounds, grazes and burns.

Prior experience with the task and knowledge of associated information needs to be established by asking the trainee. This ensures that the training is not covering old ground, and that the trainee does not lose attention, thus missing key information.

Finally, the duration of the training and the method of instruction needs to be spelt out. The trainee feels more comfortable knowing how long the session will last (as anyone subjected to an open-ended presentation will attest), and how the session will be conducted. When told that a demonstration will be followed by supervised practise, the trainee is more likely to pay attention and ask questions. Many assume that the procedure will be demonstrated only, and are surprised by a request to practise afterwards. Expectations need to be established at the start.

The introduction thus covers the same areas as the planning process:

What—What are you going to teach me?
Why—Why is it important that I follow these procedures?
How—How will I be taught?
When—When will we be finished?

Aside from putting the trainee at ease, these key elements of the introduction are necessary to set the scene for effective training.

Body of the training session

Several factors contribute to the success of the presentation or demonstration aspect of the training session, the most important of which is the animation of the trainer. A multitude of studies into training effectiveness have failed to find a single, consistent variable which contributes to training effectiveness. However, the most commonly occurring variable found to influence learning is the enthusiasm of the trainer. A number of other factors will contribute to the effectiveness of training delivery and the following questions can be asked with regard to this type of training:

Logical—Are the steps broken down into a logical process, without the trainer leaping like a grasshopper from one unrelated point to another?

Complete—Are all steps explained fully? Frequently, trainers who are overly familiar with the task make dangerous assumptions. For example, the explanation that the brake and clutch work in opposites can lead an ignorant trainee to attempt to accelerate when letting the clutch out, while changing down through the gears, around a corner. Having been told that *each* time the clutch is released, the accelerator should be depressed, this trainee did exactly as she was told, skidding and squealing around corners!

Correct—Is the trainer an expert? Some trainers teach their staff bad habits. This is ignorance compounding ignorance.

Interesting—Is the presentation interesting or motivating? Personal anecdotes, examples and stories can help to reinforce the point.

Clear—Are the procedures and knowledge explained clearly? Instructions need to be clearly presented with accompanying demonstrations. Use of simple language, explanation of terminology, and repetition all assist in the communication of key messages.

Multi-sensory—Does the presentation appeal to more than one sense (hearing, seeing, smelling, touching and tasting)? The addition of visual material to verbal instructions can improve retention by more than 50 per cent.

Multimedia—Does the trainer use more than one training aid? The use of more than one medium, such as written materials, diagrams, pictures and other aids, in addition to verbal instructions, can enhance learner understanding and improve attentiveness.

Other training issues which can enhance the value of the demonstration are:

Questioning—Are open-ended questions asked to test the trainee's understanding? 'Do you understand?' is an example of a poor, closed question. Few trainees have the courage to say 'no', since this is a reflection of the calibre of the training and the ability of the trainer to communicate effectively. Appropriate open-ended questions usually start with 'Why?', 'What?', 'When?', 'Who?' and 'How?'.

Pace—Is the presentation unhurried and uninterrupted? The pace needs to suit the trainee's ability to absorb information, neither too fast nor too slow.

Conclusion

Repetition of key steps and knowledge, with some questioning to obtain some formative feedback on the trainee's understanding, should conclude the presentation. Questions such as 'Which aspects of this are the most difficult for you?' or 'Which aspects of the demonstration would you like to have repeated?' are useful for this purpose. Note again that closed questions such as 'Was this difficult?' or 'Would you like this repeated?' are not constructive. Before allowing the trainee to practise, the trainer needs to be sure that they will succeed. Success builds confidence, so putting someone into a situation for which they are ill-prepared is demotivating and destructive. The trainer should do everything possible to ensure that a successful outcome is achieved.

PRACTICE

Immediate practice is important in the learning process. No matter how effective the presentation, unless the trainee is given the opportunity to immediately practise the skills, procedures or tasks, learning will not occur. This point needs to be stressed:

> THE EFFECTIVENESS OF TRAINING IS MEASURED BY THE
> LEARNING THAT RESULTS FROM IT.

Training is not about teaching; it is about learning. This can be illustrated with a barometer, as in Figure 8.3. In some cases there is more instruction than learning, in others more learning than instruction. Obviously the second case is the more successful.

The practice part of the training session is thus the most important part, giving the trainee the opportunity to apply the knowledge and skills taught, and giving the trainer the opportunity to assess whether the procedures or tasks can be performed to the required standard in the future. This stage of the training process enables the trainer to give positive feedback, and to supervise carefully and correct mistakes. Positive feedback should be specific and clear. 'Well done' is totally unsatisfactory. The feedback should state what the person has done correctly, and why this is important; for example, 'You were careful to place the credit card in your hand together with the receipt. That way you will ensure that the customer doesn't leave without it.' Likewise, negative feedback should state what needs to be done and why it is important in the whole process: 'When the card number isn't validated, the transaction won't be approved when processed at the bank, so

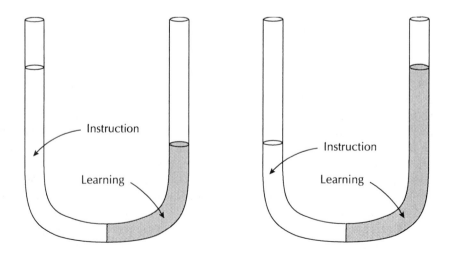

Figure 8.3   Instruction and learning

OUTLINE OF A TRAINING SESSION

Planning

What	Task analysis and writing training objectives/learning outcomes
Who	Audience—job specification and employee skills training needs analysis
When	Session time and place
How	Detailed lesson plan including equipment and aids
Why	Cost/benefit analysis

Presentation

Introduction	Trainee needs to know	• What is to be taught • Why it is important • How will I be trained? • When will we finish?
Body	Logical Complete Correct Interesting Clear Multi-sensory and multimedia Open questions to test understanding Appropriate pace	
Summary	Repetition Open questioning before practice to test readiness	

Practice

	Correction
	Objectives achieved?
	Positive feedback

remember [when taking telephone sales] to repeat the number aloud to the customer to ensure that it is one hundred per cent correct'.

Finally, the training is not complete until the trainee has been successful. It should leave the trainee feeling confident that the task could be performed without supervision. This the trainer's final responsibility: to ensure that procedures are followed and that performance standards are achieved.

The lesson (training) plan detailed here deals with the simple process of applying an adhesive dressing. This is a task which should take only a few seconds, but is used to illustrate the point that unless the trainee is given the necessary background knowledge, some tasks are either done carelessly or not at all. In many service organisations (such as hotels, airlines, restaurants, surgeries, schools, hostels, prisons and hospitals), staff face higher than average risks of being infected by diseases such as hepatitis B. With the adherence to Health and Safety Regulations (the covering of minor cuts, abrasions, grazes and burns), this risk is reduced.

LESSON PLAN: HOW LONG CAN IT TAKE TO LEARN TO APPLY AN ADHESIVE DRESSING?

STAGE	CONTENT	TEACHING POINTS	RESOURCES
Introduction	Introduction	My name is Jacki. It is my responsibility to assist you here and help you achieve the training objective, so all you have to do is relax and listen.	Name badge
	What we will do	Today I am going to teach you, as part of your first aid course, how to correctly apply an adhesive dressing.	Show adhesive dressing
	Any prior knowledge	Have you applied adhesive dressings before? Were you aware of the importance of sterile conditions when performing this task?	Can you explain what we mean when we talk about a sterile dressing?
	Objective	Today I am going to teach you to correctly apply a dressing, an adhesive dressing to be specific, so that the gauze remains sterile and the wound is protected from further abrasion and is free from germs. It is also important that the person feels comfortable once the dressing is applied.	
	When we will finish	This will take approximately 10 minutes.	
	How we will do it	First I will show you the correct procedure, second you will copy me and, third, you will attempt to do the task on your own while I watch.	Offer step-by-step written guide for future reference
	Why we will do it	The reason why we learn to do this is two-fold. It will help you every day, even when applying your own dressings. You may not be aware of the dangers of hepatitis infection through open wounds and this is why it is important to cover cuts and abrasions. This reduces the risk of cross-infection. Second, tetanus is a severe risk and can be the result of an injury while working in the garden or handling vegetables. Injuries of this nature often occur in the kitchens, cuts and burns being the most common and this is why this is so important.	Anecdotal evidence of serious infection from minor cuts and abrasions • carpet burn • rugby • gardening • kitchen

LESSON PLAN—*continued*

STAGE	CONTENT	TEACHING POINTS	RESOURCES
	Who will help if necessary	Once you have completed training you will be able to call on the first aid officer who is fully qualified if you are unsure about the extent of injuries and their treatment. He/she is available on ext. 567.	Point to wall notices for emergency
Body of Presentation	Assessing the cut or abrasion	Before applying the adhesive dressing, we need to check on two things: • is this the type of cut to which an adhesive dressing should be applied? • has the wound been properly cleaned and has an antiseptic been applied where necessary.	Pictures of wounds Q: Why is it important to clean the wound before applying a dressing? Q: What types of wounds would you not apply dressings to? Q: What would you do if you were unsure?
Tell and Show	Opening the package	When opening the package ensure that you hands are clean and that you do not drop the contents on the floor. Tear the top off Pull the red string Remove the dressing	Candidate follows actions Need several adhesive dressings for this (i.e., four)
	Prepare the patient	Rest the limb or finger on a surface to stabilise Talk to person expressing empathy Bend dressing in half to expose the tabs	
	Apply the dressing	Touching tabs only apply sterile gauze to cut, positioned to assist healing, i.e. pull skin together	Q: Why do you avoid touching the dressing?

LESSON PLAN—*continued*

STAGE	CONTENT	TEACHING POINTS	RESOURCES
		When applying to fingers, check circulation to see that it is not too tight.	For very minor cuts or very hairy people, can cut off part of the sticky part so that there is less area to adhere to hairs!
		Ask person if comfortable.	
		Advise person to keep dry and apply new dressing regularly; and what to do if healing does not occur.	Q: Why should the dressing be changed?
Practice	Ask candidate to apply dressing while explaining what they are doing	Watch the actions of the candidate carefully giving positive feedback.	Q: Why is it important to apply this correctly?
		Correct where necessary, if errors require it then ask candidate to do it a second time.	Q: In this establishment what are the circumstances in which this type of dressing may need to be applied?
		You must ensure that the candidate is 100 per cent competent.	
			Q: Which points are least clear in your mind?
Close	Revise key points	• Which dressing for which wound • Cleanliness of injury and hands • Opening and applying avoid touching gauze • Ensure person's comfort and after care	Q: How confident do you feel about doing this in future? Summary sheet Contact for you (tel.) Contact for First Aid Officer

The lesson plan, entitled 'How long can it take to learn to apply an adhesive dressing?', can be used to test against the standards suggested above. Is the training logically organised, are visual aids planned, and are the proposed questions open-ended? These criteria can be applied and possible further improvements suggested.

As anyone who has suffered an injury would know, treatment is only part of the expected service. Empathy and concern are the other dimension. This personal dimension, based on the perception of the receiver (in this case the patient), is the more complex dimension of service training to be dealt with in the next chapter. A two-dimensional view of service enables trainers in the services sector to focus on two quite different aspects of staff performance: first, the procedures to be followed; and second, the personal dimension of service. In judging performance, standard tasks are easily judged in objective terms. However, the success of the personal dimension of service (the interaction with the customer) is dependant on the subjective reaction of this customer. This is most commonly described as the 'attitude' displayed by the staff. As in our ice-skating analogy in chapter one, the procedural aspect is the technical performance, while the personal aspect is the artistic impression. Customer relations is both a science and an art, and it is to the artistic, subjective dimension of service to which we now turn.

EXERCISES AND DISCUSSION

1. Explain how to conduct a training needs analysis.

2. Why is it useful to write a training objective?

3. How you would structure the introduction to your training session?

4. Give an explanation, using your own experience, of the importance of practice.

5. How do you evaluate whether training has been successful?

9

STAFF TRAINING: further development of service competence (personal dimension of service)

SUMMARY

This chapter takes training a step further, to discuss training for the personal dimension of service. If you wish, the previous chapter covered the science of customer service; this one will cover the art of customer service. Of course, the two cannot be separated as both are an integral part of the interaction between the staff member and the customer. It is useful, however, to focus on this dimension and some other training techniques that develop the ability to self-evaluate, to enable staff to learn to learn.

CHAPTER OBJECTIVES

On completion of this chapter you will be able to:

- explain the concept of role modelling;
- use the concept of reflection on experience in training;
- train staff to adapt to different contexts and demands;
- train staff to cope with the unexpected;
- assist staff to evaluate their own performance;
- assist staff to learn from their experience.

STAFF TRAINING

Procedural training as described in the previous chapter is quite straightforward. Classical job instruction techniques require that the trainer demonstrates the procedure to the trainee, that the trainee is then given the opportunity to practise and that the trainer checks that the skills have reached a required level. In handling a credit card transaction, for example, the steps involved can be listed in sequence and the trainee taught accordingly.

Figure 9.1 highlights the personal dimension of service as distinct from the procedural dimension of service. The two dimensions are separated only because procedures lend themselves to simple task analysis and structured training, as described in the previous chapter. In contrast, the personal dimension of service is more complex, requiring employees to respond appropriately to wide-ranging customer needs and to communicate effectively in interactions with them. Developing communication competence is a life-long learning process and managers and trainers need to acknowledge this when training staff in customer relations.

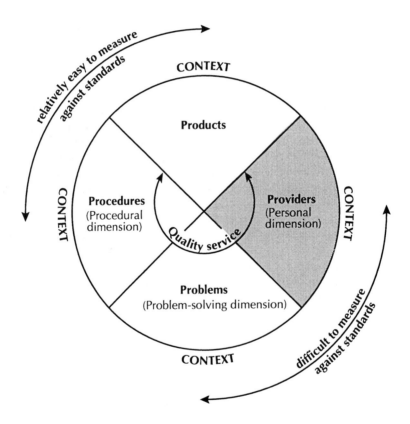

Figure 9.1   Training for the personal dimension of service

Customer relations training, or the personal dimension of service delivery, requires expertise and judgement on the part of the trainer. Assume that the trainer has years of valuable experience in the industry and extensive customer relations experience. If the trainer 'shows' the employee what good service looks like there are two possible pitfalls. The first is that the trainer has not accurately perceived the customers needs, and in fact has not delivered the best service to match the circumstances. Without checking the customer's perceptions, no-one would ever know whether the service met or exceeded the customer's expectations. At best the trainer can say 'Watch me do it, but I'm not sure that this is the best way'. Unfortunately, to escape this trap, trainers in customer relations simply critique the employee's efforts, most often lacking the confidence to demonstrate their own skills. The second pitfall is that each and every service interaction or communication is unique and that there are no simple answers, steps or procedures for these highly adaptive skills.

"YOU MAY be interested in the persistence of computer systems in our banking industry," wrote an anonymous reader when sending us an envelope from Westpac addressed: "Mr Mr J. W. Yoon Address Obsolete ... Dear Mr Address Obsolete." Doesn't a human eye ever look at material churned out by computers?

(SMH, 22/6/94)

The two problems with skills training in service provision are thus:

- without checking the customer's perceptions, how do we know that the trainer has demonstrated the best practice?
- each service interaction is unique.

It could be suggested that the first problem is solved by asking the customer. Now this idea has merit. But, generally speaking, customers hate to complain and seldom have anything negative to say even when asked directly. A recent TV show had some actors filling food service roles in a five-star hotel. These actors performed the most diabolical acts—clearing plates with their hands, leaning over the customers, being overly familiar, spilling drinks, slopping food which was served cold—and despite all this, the customers did their best to avoid confrontation.

In our society we are conditioned to avoid complaining openly, confronting verbally or suggesting improvements. Seeking feedback is a special skill which will be discussed in some detail later. The value of this feedback needs to be explained to the customer to set the right climate for full disclosure.

Returning to the training process, if we accept that each service interaction is unique, how do we go about training staff in this complex activity?

EXPERTISE

It is generally agreed that expertise is a result of many years of practice and evaluation and that supervisors and managers need to have confidence in their own expertise in the field of customer relations. (For managers who disappear as soon as the going gets tough, a course in the development of self-confidence is sorely needed!) In many service organisations, senior management are required to

INDUSTRIAL and business magnates used to boast they'd started work as Post Office telegram boys. Telegrams have gone, so now they boast about starting as mailroom boys—and girls. Australia Post, to publicise its 100th Post Shop in NSW, at 181 Castlereagh Street, held a search for the Mailroom Champ. Entrants had to be under 19—but Australia Post discovered many, many mailroom boys and girls are 40-plus. Eventually, at the George Patterson advertising agency, they found Suzanne Pal—whose boss, Alex Hamill, started, ahem, in the mailroom.

(SMH, 3/10/94)

spend several hours a week in front-line service positions. This keeps them in touch with customer needs and, more importantly, gives junior staff the opportunity to watch them in action.

In your own career you are probably able to identify people on whom you have modelled yourself. There are without doubt people whose skills you have admired and sought to emulate. These are the sort of people who remain unflustered in absolutely any situation, who treat you or the customer (internal and external) with a degree of attentiveness that implies that you have 100 per cent of their attention. You are the completely in focus, and your ideas are listened to and understood. You feel valued.

'In my experience I have watched such a person whose skills remain indelibly etched in my memory despite having watched him in action for the last time at least fourteen years ago. The charm and grace that characterised each communication with a customer or staff member were a delight to watch. These skills were consistently applied to all his daily communications, regardless of the seniority of the staff member or the importance of the customer. This calm assurance, empathy and ability to focus on others was never more clearly demonstrated than when a customer suffered a heart attack. Words cannot describe how well he handled such a difficult situation.'

Not everyone has to deal with situations like this, which are in all reality very difficult. There are crises in each and every business, and managers are the role models for the actions of staff. A negative, abrupt, non-listening approach to staff will be reflected in their communications with the customers.

TRAINING FOR SERVICE COMPETENCE

Role modelling

The first step in developing skills in customer relations is to ask the employee to watch their manager (or trainer) closely when dealing with customers. This, though, is not enough. These observations are useless unless the employee learns from them.

Knowledge acquisition

Alongside role modelling, the trainee needs to be introduced to service concepts as they apply to communication with the customer. Concepts such as: questioning, and the difference between open and closed questions; body language and its use in predicting and anticipating customer needs, especially when judging how much time the customer has available; concepts relating to offering alternatives and to closing the sale.

In addition, other types of local knowledge are important too, such as knowledge relating to different types of customer that have been gained over a period of time, or about the special needs of regular customers.

By developing the employee's knowledge base and offering the manager or trainer as a role model, the employee is able to apply these concepts to situations. An emphasis on flexibility, and the assurance that most of the time one can never be sure that the service delivered was everything it could be, will ensure that this type of training is a co-operative exercise. This will give the employee the confidence to experiment with his or her own behaviours, and to evaluate the success or otherwise of interactions with customers, both their own and that of their role model.

Reflection

Discussion after role modelling or practice is the most important feature of service skill development. 'What do you think?' is a good question to encourage the employee to look back over the behaviours exhibited in the service interaction, at the verbal and non-verbal aspects of communication, and to evaluate them. Encouraging the employee to apply concepts to the observed behaviours requires courage, but it is the only way in which they can develop their own judgement relating to quality service. Discussing the service strategies used requires an acknowledgement that there is seldom a 'correct' way to do things, that different individuals have different styles, and that customers all have different perceptions of what is quality service. And if a manager is prepared to do this, they will go a long way towards developing a flexible approach to service delivery. More importantly, it is an approach which encourages further skill development, allows for mistakes and encourages the employee to reflect on their behaviours. Developing expertise in this complex field involves assimilating concepts, knowledge and experience through a reflective and adaptive process. A true service professional will acknowledge that they learn something about customers every day. If trainees aren't doing the same, reviewing situations and learning from them with the appropriate encouragement, then they will never become successful professionals for whom good service is an art form.

This is experiential learning: using experience as the basis for developing new ideas and constructs, trying and practising new skills and constantly adapting them to new and unique situations. This level of adaptability, flexibility and willingness to change are valuable attributes in an industry in which change is essential in response to market needs.

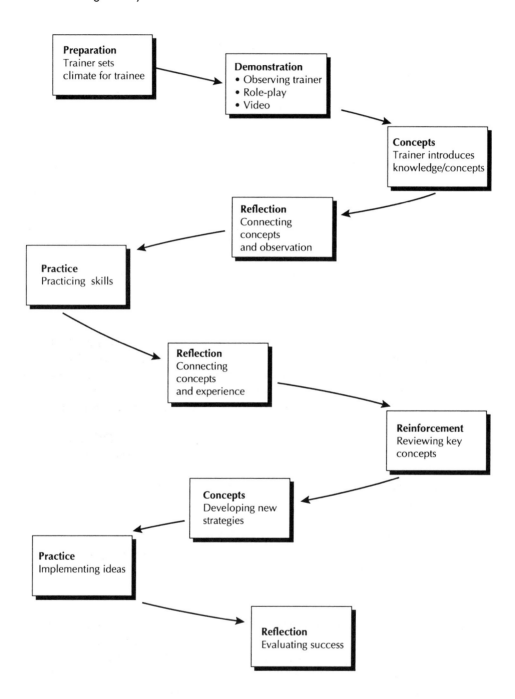

Figure 9.2   Service skill development – a lifelong progress

SERVICE SKILL DEVELOPMENT— A LIFE-LONG PROCESS

In developing skills in areas such as customer service, the following stages are suggested as part of a life-long learning process, and are shown in Figure 9.2.

Preparation

At the early stage of preparation, the manager or trainer needs to go through the same points covered in the last chapter—why the issue is important, how long the training will take and what will be achieved. The content and outcomes of this training can be negotiated, but this depends on the training context. As part of developing a quality service culture, a manager would possibly tackle the issue as a co-operative learning effort, with staff raising important issues and learning in the process of resolving these issues. In other cases, the training may be more structured, for example, when employees are new and service training is part of the induction process.

Demonstration

At this stage of the training, the service interaction needs to be demonstrated. Clearly the best context for this is a realistic work situation which the trainee observes. If this is not possible, simulations, role plays and videos can provide examples of interactions that can then be discussed during the next stage of the training. It is important that these demonstrations are as realistic as possible. They should be complex, problem-based and cover a range of issues. Humorous caricatures are seldom appropriate, as the message is generally lost in the humour. Difficult service issues are not black and white; they are grey. In order to discuss and evaluate subtle differences in behaviour, trainees need to be able to pick out these subtle differences. For this reason, role modelling in a realistic context and role plays are most appropriate for the demonstration phase.

Concepts

Following a brief discussion of the trainee's observations of the demonstration, key concepts can be introduced and related back to the observed behaviour.

Reflection

A trainee using the concepts introduced should then be encouraged to reflect upon the application of these concepts and knowledge to the observed behaviour (of both the demonstrator and customer), to past situations that they have experienced and to future situations in which they might find themselves. This is a process of making connections and seeing the relevance of the concepts introduced.

Practice

The trainee should then have an opportunity to practise skills in realistic situations. Immediately after the practice, the event should be described in detail (either verbally or in writing) before further analysis. It is very difficult to remember all verbal and non-verbal aspects of communication processes, and developing the ability to observe and recall these is an important part of the training process.

Reflection

Now that the trainee has had the opportunity to try out their skills in one or more situations, connections can be made with the earlier demonstration by the trainer and with the concepts discussed previously. Reflection, in this case, is based on the trainee's recent experience. The sooner this occurs after the event the better. If this is not possible, then a written account of what occurred can be used for later reflection and analysis.

Reinforcement

Reviewing key concepts and introducing new ones as they relate to the experience of the trainee ensures that reinforcement occurs and that new concepts are relevant and meaningful.

Concepts

Developing alternative strategies is the aim of the concepts stage of the training process. It entails brainstorming, and is a creative activity which is the basis for flexibility and continuous quality improvement.

Practice

The trainee should be given the opportunity to practise again, this time attempting new strategies. Awareness of verbal and non-verbal behaviours, both their own and that of customers, is usually enhanced at this stage, which involves further reflection and evaluation of success.

Reflection

During reflection, the trainee is better able to evaluate their success, to decide how their skills need further improvement, to find out more about issues of concern and to develop strategies for achieving personal learning goals. This is not the end of the learning process; it is the start of learning how to learn. Employees with the ability to observe closely and to learn from their daily experience are the core component of a learning culture in an organisation.

Training a staff member to be aware of and responsive to customer perceptions is thus a life-long process. This is something that can be highly rewarding, becoming more aware of the customers' perceptions, attitudes and values and matching service to these.

Unlike training on procedures, where watching a trainee do it once correctly is sufficient, training in the customer relations aspect of service is ongoing. It is, without doubt, one area in which expertise is developed over a period of time through exposure to a wide range of people and problems, and through an ability to learn from each of these interactions and to remain flexible in the ways in which one responds.

It may be helpful to look at these customer relations skills by breaking them down into smaller components. This is done with some reluctance, as there is the tendency for trainers to use these components for assessment, when quality service is something that has to be judged holistically in a given situation. Nonetheless, we could look at some of the skills mentioned earlier and develop a chart for feedback purposes, allowing the observation of service delivery in a range of different situations. No doubt these could be tailored to the types of situations most frequently encountered in all organisations.

SERVICE CIRCUMSTANCES—SITUATIONS IN WHICH SERVICE IS GIVEN

Service is given in a wide variety of situations to a variety of people:

Peak periods
Quiet periods
One or two customers waiting
Regular customers
New customers
Elderly customers
Customers with language difficulties
Customers who won't stop talking
Customers who take up time but never spend
Young customers
Customers in a hurry
Customers with impossible children
Loud and/or abusive customers.

When dining out, it has been shown that (on the whole) attentiveness at the start of the meal is more important than at the end. The exception to this is undoubtedly the family with young children which needs prompt service throughout the meal for their own sanity as well as the sanity of others in the restaurant. However, customers will tolerate delays over bill paying which they would not tolerate at the start of the meal. These initial interactions need to be prioritised, and newly arrived customers need to be given immediate attention. In a bank, the egalitarian ideal remains strong—attending to a late arrival, however quickly, will cause a riot in the queue. Shop attendants will sometimes leave one customer to help another who appears to have a fast transaction, and then return to the first. This skill

LUNCHING yesterday, Ahmad Akbar, of Beecroft, splashed soy sauce all over his shirt—and he had an important meeting to go to. Solution: Straight to DJ's Market Street store and pay $49.95 for a new business shirt. There was still a worry—the new shirt had creases, and did the salesman, Nicholas, know where it could be ironed? Yes, indeed. Nicholas took it to the staff rooms, ironed it, and had it back in a few minutes, no charge.
(*SMH*, 19/7/94)

in reading the needs of both customers is valuable, but even the most experienced salesperson can find themselves in trouble for attempting to facilitate in this way. In all service situations, staff must make an instantaneous evaluation of the approach they plan to take with the customer and this, in part, depends on the circumstances.

In each situation, the employee also has to utilise a range of skills. These include the ability to judge when it is appropriate to intervene when a customer has not asked for assistance. Often a customer will give the impression that assistance is not necessary, yet a second offer, recommendation or direct question will open up the service interaction and avoid the customer walking out the door without communicating with the staff in a meaningful way.

SERVICE SKILLS DISPLAYED

We could atomise service behaviours further than that detailed in the early chapters of this book, but as an author I am fearful that future managers and trainers will use these ideas to develop checklists for assessment purposes. My advice is 'Don't!' Not every one of these behaviours will be demonstrated in each service situation. As the circumstances for service delivery demand flexibility, training demands flexibility in the assessment of competence. It cannot be stressed enough that an ability to demonstrate flexibility in assessing competence in the service context is one of the most important attributes as a trainer. Expert judgement and careful analysis of the context and behaviours exhibited, in partnership with the trainee, is the only way to develop their ability to deliver professional service.

If a situation is going to be judged holistically, we might then ask why such emphasis has been placed on atomistically listing some service behaviours? This is because most feedback given to staff is unhelpful. 'That was good' is not adequate for performance feedback. In comparison, 'I was watching the way you listened so attentively to the last customer. He was really having a difficulty expressing himself, wasn't he? Your patience paid off, since you managed to offer him exactly what he wanted and close the sale. I'm sure he will be back again' is more like it. By using some of the service constructs listed in this book, you can give feedback that is more meaningful.

DESCRIPTIVE FEEDBACK IS FOUND BY MANY TRAINERS AND TRAINEES TO BE FAR MORE HELPFUL THAT CHECKLISTS AND CHARTS.

So far, two aspects of service competence have been tackled. These are the skills, such as the ability to listen attentively, and the circumstances in which these skills are applied. From the employee's point of view, some knowledge relating to service concepts

A PAINED cry from Wendy Whiteman, on the switch at Grace Bros' city store, to say they give great service, too, just like David Jones ... Early this year, a woman from San Diego, California, asked for a Driza-Bone coat. They don't stock Driza-Bone, but "Mozzie" Norris later went to Gowing's, bought one there and mailed it to San Diego. Three months later, she wrote back—it didn't fit, so could GBs exchange it? "Mozzie" bought a better size, but didn't post it. He was planning a visit to the US so put the Driza-Bone in his luggage, and even now may be exchanging it in San Diego to keep a customer satisfied.
(SMH, 26/7/94)

would also be most helpful. One needs to remember that the ultimate aim of customer relations training is developing the employee's judgement of the appropriate ways to respond to customers. To do this, the employee needs to develop these constructs, such as active listening and open questioning, to evaluate his or her own service delivery. The trainer's aim should be to develop the trainee's ability to judge the success or otherwise of service interactions. By presenting role models and discussing the situation after the event, these concepts can be used to analyse and review the situation. Likewise, when the employee attempts to develop customer relations skills, they should be encouraged to evaluate the service delivery and to learn and adapt the concepts to the next situation encountered.

This method of experiential learning is aimed at having the employee take ownership of behaviour and to reflect on the success or otherwise of communication with others. In doing so, they are able to develop self-awareness and achieve intrinsic satisfaction. Based on the service constructs introduced to the employee, reflection on the communication with the customer should enable them to self-evaluate. This is an important principle of adult learning and is the key to developing autonomous staff who are able to engage in a constant process of service delivery and evaluation of quality.

CONTEXT OF SERVICE—POTENTIAL VALUE TO THE ORGANISATION

If we wanted to add a yet another aspect of service performance, it would relate to the importance of the interaction with the client, customer or staff member (internal customer). For example, if we were to contrast the sale of an hotel room to a free independent traveller (FIT, as they are known in the trade) with the sale of ninety rooms on a special deal during the hotel's lowest period of occupancy, clearly the demands of the second situation exceed those of the first. In both situations, the same skills are potentially used, the circumstances are different (such as a new FIT client) but now the third dimension, the degree of importance of the service delivered, is added. If there is a lot at stake in terms of income or future business, then this dimension could be useful. You might argue that every interaction or communication in the delivery of quality service is as important as the next. However, salary rates paid to the Marketing Manager in comparison to the front-line service personnel belies this.

The contexts in terms of potential value to the business are, for example,

Potential for revenue—depending on what the customer's business is worth, the salesperson would be expected to spend far more time on a big sale than a small one, and the customer expects this too;

Potential for further business—although this is a small sale, it may lead to future dealings, which is the case with most customers;

Potential for recommendation—the customer may be have profound effect on business through recommendations, such as in the media, or may simply tell a range of other clients about the level of service offered.

In a busy work environment, employees are constantly making decisions about who to serve next, who to call next, who to give priority to and which task to tackle. This aspect of service delivery aims to acknowledge the varied importance of interactions with customers and to enable staff to allocate their time appropriately. Time is a scarce resource, and prioritisation is a key element of work organisation.

To review these ideas, it may be useful to reconsider the diagram of service delivery (Figure 1.2), in which context—in addition to the procedural and personal dimensions of service—was illustrated.

MERGING THE DIMENSIONS OF SERVICE

Clearly the two dimensions of service—procedural and personal—cannot be separated any more than the technical marks can be separated from the artistic impression in ice-skating. To succeed, the service provider needs to do well in both aspects. Errors in the procedural aspect can lead to goods being delivered to the wrong address, the wrong sized being ordered, the wrong form being completed, credit being given when it should not, credit being refused when it should not, and so on. The development of company policies and procedures ensures that the customer's process requirements are met: in an hotel the room is ready, the bathroom clean and the food hot. But these are not the only reasons why people visit hotels; the ambience, the attitude of the staff and other more subjective factors are a substantial part of the motivation for leaving home. Surveys of people eating out reveal that, in nearly every case, 'atmosphere' is what patrons are looking for and enjoying. An escape from the normal environment, exposure to new faces and a guarantee that staff will have a pleasant, friendly demeanour are key elements contributing to the motivation to dine out. Likewise, many shoppers really enjoy shopping. It provides an opportunity to go into a different environment, to see and do things that are new. For many people, shopping is a cheap form of entertainment (the money was going to be spent anyway), and retailers who perceive the importance of providing innovative shopping experiences are likely to make big profits in the future. At present, entertainment is provided to lure children and to keep them busy while parents are spending. The next step would be to provide entertainment for other market segments in order to turn a chore into an event.

In the customer's mind the two facets of the service are merged, with the final holistic perception being of 'good service' or 'bad service'. In the same way, an holistic judgement needs to be made of the service interaction assessed by a trainer. Whatever the trainer's assessment of the demonstrated quality of service, for the employee to *learn* this judgement should not be made entirely by the trainer: the employee is an adult learner, and thus an authoritarian approach of 'telling' them about their service delivery is counterproductive. Instead, to foster a learning approach to service skill development, the employee needs to participate in making these judgements, so developing ownership of the situation and the ability to transfer this learning to future situations.

The feedback process

The case study dialogue provided as an example of a feedback process illustrates how a trainer can assist an employee to reflect on their experience and reach their own judgements regarding quality dimensions. The trainer has made no evaluative remarks whatsoever, but has only directed the employee's attention to certain factors and reinforced key points. This process of reflection on experience is the most important part of the learning process, and the one seriously neglected in most cases. It is extremely time consuming, since a judgement by the trainer would be made along the following lines: 'Your questioning was good, but you forgot to greet the customer that was waiting, and you should be wearing the correct uniform.' This is not productive; it is the employee that needs to acknowledge these factors, to take ownership of them and to learn how to learn from experience.

The biggest barrier to learning from experience is the lack of time spent on the process of thinking about situations that have occurred and reaching conclusions. Very seldom is adequate time allocated to this most important stage of the training process. The evaluation of service interactions with customers need not occur immediately after the event, although the communication process is easier to remember if recalled soon after the customer has gone. The process can occur some time later in recalling critical incidents. This entails recalling incidents which have been particularly problematic, reviewing them and using them to evaluate alternative strategies. Use of critical incidents can produce a rich training resource, a wide range of incidents which are relevant to the learner which can be used to enhance the learning process.

CASE STUDY—ENCOURAGING SELF-EVALUATION AND OWNERSHIP OF PERFORMANCE
Greeting and assisting a client with an enquiry: a dialogue

TRAINER
The assessment you have just finished is for the competency element 'Greeting and assisting a client with an enquiry'. What aspects of the interaction do you think went particularly well?

EMPLOYEE
Well, I thought that I asked a lot of questions to find out what she wanted.

Yes, you used a lot of questions. Were they open or closed questions?

Let me think, yes, the question that really started her off was 'What are you going to be using the computer for?'

That was an excellent question, since it allowed you to offer specific solutions to her problems. This allows both you and your customer to save time and ensure that her needs were more closely met. Were there any other aspects which you think went particularly well?

I can't think of any.

If you were to think about the body language in the communication you had with the customer, both your's and their's, what would you notice?

Well, I walked out from behind the counter to show her the brochures.

And what about your customer? Was there anything you noticed about her body language or other non-verbal factors?

She seemed very relaxed. She obviously had plenty of time to spend on her decision. I didn't have all day, though!

The time spent with each customer always varies, doesn't it?

It is hardest when you are busy and they want to take their time.

How did you handle the timing with this customer?

Well, that was the difficult part. She had to wait for a few minutes while I finished helping someone else. Then just when I could give her my full attention two other customers arrived. And we had been quiet all morning!

I was about to ask you to reflect on what you might do differently if you were to do this again. Is this one of the things you would look at?

Yes, I thought afterwards that I should have smiled and told her that I wouldn't be long. I have lost customers before when they get tired of waiting. If you apologise to them for the delay and promise to help them, they are often prepared to wait for longer.

Acknowledging waiting customers is important. How does the customer you are serving react to the interruption?

Very few worry about it, and they often speed up their own requests if they are aware that someone is waiting.

Is there anything else that you would do differently?

I don't think so.

We have been talking about non-verbal communication, and uniform is part of the image that we present to customers ...

Oh, yes. I'm sorry I didn't wear the correct shirt today: my long-sleeve one was in the wash. I suppose that uniform is important?

A very important part of the customer's perception of our business. Can you think of any situations in which you have been a customer and noticed the uniforms?

I guess I've noticed airline crews. They always look perfect.

Would you like to summarise what we have said?

Well, I asked a few open-ended questions which helped me to find out what the customer wanted, and I left my counter to help her on the floor. I forgot, though, to acknowledge the other customers that were waiting and I am not wearing the right uniform.

How was this feedback and discussion helpful to you?

Well, it helped me to see aspects of my communication with customers. I always do these things without thinking, and this made me more aware of what I am doing and how I can improve.

During the feedback process, the employee should be encouraged to think carefully about the communication process and to review strategies, evaluate them and possibly suggest alternatives. The trainer's role in this is that of facilitator.

THE TRAINER'S ROLE IS NOT TO **GIVE** FEEDBACK, BUT TO **ENCOURAGE** REFLECTION.

With this approach, flexibility is developed along with analytical skills that will enhance future communications. Employees learn to learn. This, the feedback loop, forms the basis for total quality management.

Certainly many service outcomes are intangible, but having processes in place to obtain customer feedback, to modify and adapt service accordingly will ensure quality outcomes for both employees and customer. Customer and staff satisfaction are the aims of a twin approach to quality management.

EXERCISES AND DISCUSSION

1. Explain how you can approach training for dealing with unique situations.

2. What is role modelling? Can you remember any people on whom you have modelled your own behaviour?

3. In what way is a knowledge of concepts useful in training staff for customer service roles?

4. The critical incident is a suggested method for providing material for reflection in the experiential learning process. How would you use this method in running a training session? Develop a full-scale plan for a training session in which trainees discuss critical incidents in customer service.

5. Read the case study again and describe how the employee achieves ownership of performance and self-evaluation.

PERSONAL DIMENSION OF SERVICE REVIEW

Read this before your discussion with your trainer: its aim is to make you more aware of the communication that takes place when dealing with customers.

After dealing with your customer—

1. Try to recall word for word some of the things you said to the customer.

_____

_____

_____

_____

_____

2. Try to recall some of the non-verbal factors in your communication, such as timing, body language, voice qualities, use of space etc.

_____

_____

_____

_____

_____

3. Try to recall word for word some of the things the customer said.

_____

_____

_____

4. Try to recall some of the non-verbal factors in the customer's communication, such as timing, body language, voice qualities, use of space.

_____

_____

_____

_____

_____

5. What do you think your customer was thinking as he/she departed?

_____

_____

_____

_____

_____

6. Given the opportunity to talk to the same customer again, is there anything you would ask, do or say?

_____

_____

_____

_____

_____

_____

10

STAFF TRAINING: problem-solving dimension of service

SUMMARY

This chapter extends concepts introduced in chapter nine to dealing with staff training for problem-solving. While problem-solving is, like all service, a combination of procedure and personality, it is useful for services sector managers to be able to focus specifically on this aspect. Some general guidelines for problem-solving are suggested, although the context may determine that other strategies may be more appropriate. Managers and trainers need to keep this in mind.

CHAPTER OBJECTIVES

On completion of this chapter you will be able to:

- select an appropriate problem-solving strategy taking contextual factors into account;
- apply a stage-by-stage process to problem-solving;
- use effective listening skills;
- evaluate problem-solving effectiveness in the context of customer service.

STAFF TRAINING

In the first chapter, quality was described from the customer's viewpoint: the quality of the product, the quality of the procedural aspects of service, and the quality of the personal aspects of the service. To illustrate this point, drink dispensing by a robotic bartender is procedure-perfect. The quality of the product, Scotch whisky, depends on the skill and talent of the master blender, and on the possibility that the product has been watered down somewhere along the line. If it is assumed that the product is a twelve-year-old Scotch whisky of the best quality, high standards of quality service on the dimensions of product and procedure will have been achieved. However, a bar staffed by robotic drink dispensers offers little conviviality, the personal dimension of service delivery.

This personal dimension is arguably the most important factor if the primary motivation for seeking the service is the atmosphere or ambience of the pub. Somehow drinking at home is not quite the same. On the other hand, when travelling around the world, some people would prefer procedure-perfect service delivery, if this assured that destinations were reached safely and on time. No amount of charm

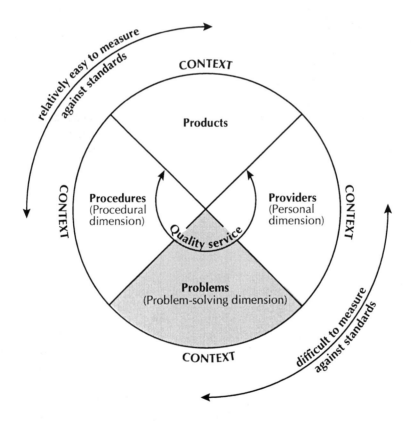

Figure 10.1 Training for problem-solving

THE CALTEX twin service centre on the F3 at Wyong is huge, but can be pretty quiet in the dead hours of the morning. Not at 3 am yesterday, however, when Jenny and Neil Crouch, of Gorokan, drove into the southbound area—she was in labour and they knew they wouldn't make the hospital. Operator Marcus Pink and Neil delivered a baby boy within five minutes—all of it captured on the security video cameras.

(*SMH*, 23/7/94)

or graciousness or personal attention or extra effort on the part of the crew can make up for delays or near-misses on landing! But if all providers of the same service are matched on price and can ensure the same standards of safety, then the personal dimension of the service provision can mean the difference between, say, success and failure of an airline. A focus on the customer through 'moments of truth' led to the outstanding success of Scandinavian Airlines in recent times.

In this book, little time has been spent on the quality of the product, since such quality is more easily and more objectively judged. Tour packages, bank loans, insurance policies, meals, flights and many other products need to be evaluated in terms of the customer's perspective of quality. Market research can be most useful in doing this. From the training viewpoint, the procedural and personal dimensions of service delivery have mainly been dealt with. In doing so, these have been further teased out into steps (in the case of procedures), and into various contexts and skills (in the case of the personal dimension). Becoming atomistic is dangerous and has led to much criticism of the behaviourist approach to objective setting. Splitting hairs is not appropriate for the personal dimension of service. Communication skills cannot be seen in isolation: listening is something that always occurs but cannot be dealt with as a single issue any more than facial expression can. For this reason, it is most important to merge these factors—steps, contexts, skills—for a more holistic view of service quality. At the same time, this view is not a judgement of the trainer, nor a judgement of the employee. Service quality is judged by the customer. The customer's perception of the product and of service is highly personal and variable, being influenced by a multitude of factors such as previous experience, mood and cultural differences. Staff training in customer relations needs to have this as its focus at all times.

PROBLEM-SOLVING

One aspect of customer service that has not yet been addressed in detail is that of problem-solving. Although problem-solving is based on both the procedural and personal dimensions of service, it has been given its own dimension because it is such an important part of service. This is shown in Figure 10.1. Problem-solving is all about dealing with the unexpected. We can't anticipate the problems a customer might have! In this chapter's case study, a problem has emerged as a result of the customer's error. There can be many other sources of problems: misunderstandings, unrealistic expectations, product faults, servicing problems or procedural delays to name but a few. The Americans with their positive approach have been known to call problems 'opportunities'. Indeed, in many cases a problem does provide the

Mark Day

The next time you get lumbered with a crappy product or service that fails to live up to its price or hype, do your country a service: Complain.

Most of us don't. We're chickens. We take the easy way out. We don't want to offend, or make a scene.

Even if the food is awful, we tend to say something like "very nice, thanks" when the waiter intrudes with the obligatory but unwelcome question about whether you're enjoying your dinner.

We just cop it. And in doing so we're allowing the second rate to become the norm.

This must change if we are to meet the challenges of the '90s and beyond.

But how? We are all resistant to change and, goodness knows, we've been subjected to enough of it in the past decade or so.

Change can only be successful if the reasons for it are understood and supported by the people at the coal face of any business.

It's simply not enough for the head of a company to decree that change must take place. Unless the change is "owned" by the people who put it into practice it will wither and die like any other good idea at the time.

So, complaining is a good idea. If enough people complain it forces product or service managers to wonder if they should change their product or the way they support it.

I get into trouble when I do it because my wife hates offending people or "making a scene." For some odd reason, she prefers to complain to me about our high-priced products which fail.

Like the microwave which has had two faulty control panels replaced, or the gas cooktop which resolutely refuses to light. Or the CD player which has had three trips to the repair shop for the same problem. Or the car radio which cost $250 to repair—and developed the same fault three weeks later.

I constantly grizzle to the repairers: Why pay through the nose for supposedly quality products when they are demonstrably inferior?

All I want is quality service. All I get is shrugs and bills. If more of us were prepared to complain—and do it loudly—a revolution would sweep this country.

And that's why the Inbound Tourism Organisation of Australia has launched the AussieHost program. It's designed to make us realise that everyone, including the nation, can profit from better service.

In Australia the visitor industry—tourism—is our No 1 foreign exchange earner, contributing $8.2 billion dollars in earnings. Almost three million visitors come from overseas each year, but they represent just 30 per cent of the industry total.

Seventy per cent of the hospitality industry's revenue comes from Australians—day trippers, interstate visitors, holidaying Australians discovering their own country.

We do not enjoy a good reputation for service. We are too often seen as lazy, apathetic, disinterested, surly, and unhelpful.

The AussieHost program is designed to change that. It has been adapted from successful similar schemes in Canada and New Zealand, and it attacks the problem from the bottom up.

Sure, prime ministers, premiers and tourism ministers can all exhort us to do better, but the program recognises that we'll only achieve better service if those who are dealing with the public every day want to do better.

AussieHost invites organisations to put their staff through a one-day course on how to improve customer relations. It presents research which shows 68 per cent of customers stopped dealing with firms because they felt they were receiving indifferent service.

They highlighted the real cost of a complaining customer.

The average business never hears from 96 per cent of its unhappy customers. They just cop sub-standard products or services and vow never to do business with that firm again.

For every complainer, therefore, we have about 26 who feel the same but don't bother to register a complaint.

Unhappy customers tell between eight and 20 other people of their experiences. So every complaint can represent about 500 people hearing negative stories about a business.

Given that it costs about six times as much to attract a new customer than it does to keep an existing customer, it is much cheaper to resolve a problem than to seek new victims.

The AussieHost program is all about better customer service.

One of the sales reps in my radio business did the course and was so enthused she sent me full details and recommended it should be compulsory for all our people.

The course is aimed at building strong communication (listening as well as speaking) skills, while instilling professionalism and pride in our work.

The key is that its objectives are "owned" by the participants.

As we move into the second half of the decade and see the number of overseas visitors swell to an Olympics 2000 crescendo, we have to ask ourselves what impressions of Australia we want them to leave with.

A "she'll be right" country? A "near enough is good enough" country? A "that's the way we do it 'ere, mate" country? A "if you don't like it, lump it" country?

Not in my book. If we adopt that attitude we know more than two-thirds of them won't come back. And they'll each tell dozens of others about us.

We'll be bad-mouthed to tens of millions of potential customers. On that basis, we'll be doing our country a service if we complain now, and force a fundamental rethink among those business managers who are content to allow sloppy, sub-standard products or services. As AussieHost says: Better service is better business.

• *AussieHost can be contacted on (02) 332-3416.*

(*Daily Telegraph Mirror, 5/7/94*)

opportunity to get a customer on side for life, if approached correctly and solved to everyone's satisfaction. (It must be said, though, that being confronted with 'opportunities' every day is not much fun!)

The problem-solving process is generally divided into stages:

Stage I—Expression of regret
Stage II—Problem clarification
Stage III—Solution generation
Stage IV—Implementation
Stage V—Follow-up

Let us review each of these in detail.

Stage I—Expression of regret

The first stage is a stumbling block for many staff, one of whom in the *Sydney Morning Herald*'s 'Column 8' extract here was heard to say on the public address system, 'The train will be delayed ... I don't apologise because I'm not the one responsible'. Many staff members unfortunately adopt this attitude. What they fail to understand is that an apology is not an admission of fault but an expression of regret that the person has suffered some inconvenience. Perhaps some would find it easier to say 'I regret that this has happened to you'. Japanese customers/visitors have been known to frequently comment on this: as one of the world's most polite nations, they expect that some empathy is expressed in the form of a sincere apology when something goes wrong. There is no need to accept blame or to cast blame. An apology is simply an expression of regret, and a desire to remedy the fault.

The *Oxford English Dictionary* defines 'sorry' as 'pained at or regretful or repentant over something, feeling pity for some one'. After giving a lengthy explanation of a problem, the last thing the customer wants a staff member to say is 'Yes?', with the tone indicating incredulous denial of a problem and the inference 'And so what do you want me to do about it?' The simple words 'I'm sorry that this has happened' are quite satisfactory as long as the tone is sincere.

ENGLISH visitor Richard Drew, after a trip to the Blue Mountains one day this week, caught the train back to Katoomba. It had its own on-line entertainment. The guard's voice came over the PA as they headed for Sydney: "I don't know what's going on—there are freight trains everywhere." Later: "The train will be delayed—we're on the wrong track. I don't apologise because I'm not the one responsible." Finally, at Strathfield: "Apologies for the delay but it wasn't my fault." (SMH, 13/6/94)

Stage II—Problem clarification

The next stage of problem-solving is clarification. Problems are so often solved by listening, with no further action necessary. This is particularly the case when the staff member is the last in a succession of frustrations. Effective listening is necessary at this stage to explore the problem. The difference between hearing and listening is illustrated in this customer's observation, 'Some staff hear what you say, others listen to you.' Hearing is the recognition of audible sounds. A dog can hear, but does he listen? Staff can hear, but do they listen? Listening is defined as the psychological experience of associating meaning with sounds. Where the meaning evolving out of the listening process is that which the customer intended, this is careful empathic listening.

Bolton (1987) groups listening skills into three clusters (attending, following and reflecting), each with their own specific skills, as shown in Table 1.

Attending

Attending involves giving full attention, particularly through the use of non-verbal behaviours such as eye contact, leaning forward, open gestures and posture, and nodding. Indicators of non-attention include shifting the feet, wandering eyes, shuffling paperwork, turning away, slouching or glazed eyes.

Removing physical barriers can also influence attending skills. Bullet-proof glass in banks offers little encouragement to customers, large desks prove intimidating to other staff (internal customers) and high reception counters infer superiority in five star hotels. The aim of listening, even at the stage of attending, is to develop empathy and demonstrate warmth.

Table 1.   Group listening skills (Bolton 1987, p. 33)

Skill clusters	Specific skills
Attending skills	• A Posture of Involvement • Appropriate Body Motion • Eye Contact • Nondistracting Environment
Following skills	• Door Openers • Minimal Encouragers • Infrequent Questions • Attentive Silence
Reflecting Skills	• Paraphrasing • Reflecting Feelings • Reflecting Meanings (Tying Feelings to Content) • Summative Reflections

Following

These skills include encouraging the person to talk further with 'minimal encouragers' (Bolton 1987) by offering attentive silence to allow the person time to talk (the opposite being interrupting) and by asking infrequent questions.

Reflecting

Reflecting has the very positive effect of showing that someone is listening well enough to remember what has been said. It can be a reflection of content (what they think the person said) or feeling (what they think the person felt). This, in addition to affirming attention and effort to understand, allows for the other person to confirm the perceived understanding. Further, it encourages the person to talk more. Taken to extremes, however, one can sound like a parrot which can be most irritating, so it should be used judiciously.

Open questions

One of the most powerful defusers in any problem situation is giving the person the opportunity to let off steam. Unless given the opportunity to do this, someone who is really angry will not listen to alternatives or solutions. The situation needs to be defused with careful attending, reflecting and asking open questions. These are questions which enable the person to elaborate, such as 'Could you please describe to me what happened in detail?' All 'What?', 'When?', 'Why?', 'Where?' and 'How?' questions tend to be open questions.

Stage III—Solution generation

In every situation there tend to be a number of solutions, and the best of these needs to be chosen to resolve the situation—and, of course, 'best' is something the customer decides. Where, for example, a credit card purchase is refused, alternatives could be offered immediately. 'I'm sorry, we were unable to authorise this credit card. Do you have some other form of payment, such as a cheque or cash?' Or 'I'm afraid we have a maintenance problem [probably a poor excuse for overbooking; an ethical issue here] with your suite. We can offer you a standard room at a substantially reduced rate or arrange a suite with a neighbouring hotel.'

Asking the customer what they would like to have done about the problem can yield some good results: 'I'd like it replaced, please' or 'I'll manage with it the way it is, but I thought you would like to know about product faults'. In some cases, this is dangerous, particularly where the customer suggests an alternative that is impossible or difficult to achieve. For example, something valuable is reported to have gone missing from a guest's room and the manager was sure that no staff had entered the room (because of a computerised key system), a question about what the guest wanted done might lead to the suggestion that the police are called. On the other hand, if the key system had been patiently explained, someone had accompanied the guest to the room to assist with the search, and mild questioning had explored some alternative locations for the missing object, the situation could be defused more easily than having uniformed officers in the lobby.

Stage IV—Implementation

The fourth stage of the problem-solving process involves taking prompt action. Timing is most important here, as delays imply a lack of concern. The person responding to the problem should be able to solve it (see the discussion in chapter fifteen on empowerment) without recourse to more senior staff, unless it is particularly serious.

Stage V—Follow-up

The last stage of the process entails checking later to see that the customer is happy with the outcome. Have you ever had anything replaced and then had the store ring to find out if it was working right? For the investment of a phone call during a quiet period, the impact this would have on a customer would be enormous. Imagine a restaurant calling to ask if a recent patron had enjoyed her birthday there. What if the restaurant dropped her a line just before the next one? The feedback phase of the customer service loop is one of the most neglected. And it provides a real *opportunity* to win a customer for life.

TRAINING AND ASSESSING PROBLEM-SOLVING SKILLS

The guidelines given here for problem-solving are just that: guidelines. As any expert knows, all problem situations are different. Some require immediate decisive action. Imagine going through this process if there was a fire ('Well, how did it start? What shall we do about it?') or if two patrons were fighting in the bar. In such cases, the staff member makes the decision and implements it immediately, after some very rapid consideration of the alternatives.

The most important part of the problem-solving process is the one not discussed so far, relating to learning. As in the previous chapter, the aim of managers (and trainers) in service industries is to create a learning culture, to develop life-long learning. In order to do this, these types of problems need to be analysed carefully after the event. A form for this purpose is provided at the end of this chapter. It is only intended as a guide, as not every event can be analysed in this way, and nor should it be. Life is full of surprises, and this is the joy of working with people every day. They surprise others time and time again. How does one train their staff to deal with the surprising and the unexpected? If nothing else, will they be encouraged to reflect on their experience, and explore alternatives?

And, finally, as a trainer how are you to assess performance on these non-routine aspects of customer service? Take a checklist-type approach? Or use a format such as the one provided? Or again, simply use holistic, descriptive feedback? Or will staff be empowered to do their own learning? Will the organisation encourage a learning culture with the intrinsic rewards associated with self-development?

EXERCISES AND DISCUSSION

1. Study the following case study and, assuming that you were John, complete the post-problem-solving analysis form provided.

    ### Case study—The floral dress with a PIN problem
    The woman, wearing a floral dress stretched taut across her ample frame, marched up to the bank's enquiries counter and thumped the bell. She appeared to be one of those people for whom assertiveness training would never be necessary. Judging by the reluctance of the staff on the floor to get up from their desks and assist her, she was the type of person that see to it that anyone in a service capacity is constantly reminded of their inferior status and obligation to please.

    Following glances from the rest of the staff, John realised that it was his turn, and that hiding behind the rubber plant was not going to get him anywhere with his colleagues. Walking briskly to the desk, and straightening his shoulders, he immediately observed that the woman's facial expression was ominous. Despite this he greeted her normally,

'Good morning, may I help you?'

'My new card doesn't work. I went shopping last night and, with a trolley full of groceries I had bought, found that I could not pay for them because my "PIN number" didn't work!' she replied with an accusatory tone.

Floored somewhat by this and wondering which approach to take, John was spared an answer by her continued explanation which was delivered at a volume loud enough to attract the attention of a number of other customers.

'I have had this account for years, and was issued with a new card as the old one had expired.' Warming up still further, she went on to describe her humiliation and anger in front of a queue of shoppers.

'I've never been so embarrassed in all my life. It was after the bank had closed and I had no other method of payment. I had to abandon all my bags of shopping. I will be writing to the papers about this. This is the second problem I've had with this bank.'

Realising that it was time that he seized the initiative, John asked whether she had tried the card in the ATM machine. Further angered by this suggestion that she hadn't attempted the obvious, the woman hit the counter with the palm of her hand and informed him that she had tried it three times and the machine had finally 'eaten' her card.

Faced with the prospect of retrieving the card from the machine or questioning her further, John felt inclined to find the card first, but realising that left alone, she could become even more excitable in his absence, decided to persevere.

'Perhaps, if you could give me your name, I could check our records of your account.'

This she provided and within a few minutes John was able to ascertain that there was a joint account held with her husband and an individual account.

'It would appear that you have a joint account with your husband, account number 8943329. Is this correct?'

'Yes, that's right, and my old "PIN number" simply doesn't work. How can this happen?'

'Could you please write on this slip your personal identification number, ma'am?'

Discovering that this was the wrong PIN for the joint account, John then checked the other, individual account. He found the card being used was for the joint account, but that the PIN was for the individual account. On further questioning, it transpired that the woman was unaware that cards were issued for the joint account and certainly could not remember having been issued with one ('Her husband wouldn't let her use it!'). In any case, when the new card arrived, she assumed that it replaced the card for her own account and promptly cut up her old one.

Embarrassed by all this, the volume of her voice dropped, but still shocked by her obvious stupidity, she remained angry that it would take a week to replace the card that she had inadvertently destroyed. Reassuring her that it was an easy mistake to make and that he would see to the request for a new card, John was relieved to see her hurry out of the bank, her body language an odd mixture of embarrassment and arrogance.

2. Recall a past incident you would describe as needing problem-solving skills. Analyse the situation (using the analysis form if useful) and decide what you learnt from the incident and what you might do differently in future if faced a similar problem.

3. How can one encourage staff to develop their problem-solving skills in the area of customer service?

4. The context in which the problem occurs is an important factor (for example, urgency). Can you think of other contextual factors that might influence your approach to solving a problem?

POST-PROBLEM-SOLVING ANALYSIS

How did the problem come to your attention?

_____

_____

How was it first expressed?

_____

_____

I Expression of regret   *What was your first reaction? (Try to remember exactly what you said and did)*

_____

_____

II Problem clarification   *How did you discover the full extent of the problem? (Describe your listening and questioning approach)*

_____

_____

What did this reveal?

_____

_____

How did the customer react at this stage?

_____

_____

III Solution generation   *What solutions were generated?*

_____

_____

_____

Which solution was chosen as appropriate? Why?

_____

_____

_____

IV   Implementation   _How was the solution implemented?_

_____

_____

_____

V   Follow-up   _Were you able to follow up on the solution implementation._

_____

_____

_____

In the end, how did the customer feel about the problem and its resolution?

_____

_____

_____

What did you learn from this event?

_____

_____

_____

How will you approach similar situations in future?

_____

_____

_____

11

COMPETENCY-BASED TRAINING AND CAREER DEVELOPMENT

SUMMARY

This chapter deals with competency standards and competency-based training in more detail than earlier chapters. As a form of systematic performance appraisal, assessment of competence is a means of quality assurance that at the same time enables the individual concerned to receive certification. An integrated, holistic view of competence, with judgement of performance by experts against standards, is suggested as the basis for appraisal and career development.

CHAPTER OBJECTIVES

On completion of this chapter you will be able to:

- define competency;
- differentiate between industry, cross-industry and enterprise standards;
- explain how competency standards can be implemented and achieved;
- list the benefits of competency-based systems.

COMPETENCY-BASED TRAINING
AND CAREER DEVELOPMENT

Training reform in Australia and in many other countries has led to the development of competency standards for industries. The implementation of competency standards and their implications these for organisations are reviewed in this chapter.

To review our earlier definition, *competency* is the ability to perform the activities within an occupation or function to the standard expected in employment.

A competency standard is comprised of units, each with an associated performance criteria. This is illustrated in Figure 11.1 and in the reproduced Hospitality Management competency unit.

Opposite page: *Hospitality Management—National Competency Standards*, Tourism Training Australia, 1994, p. 20

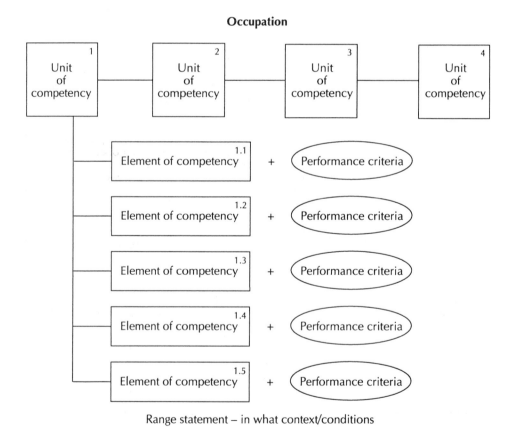

Occupation

Figure 11.1   Competency standards model

Unit Develop and Maintain Service Quality	MC12

Range of Variables:
- This unit applies to all occupational streams in the hospitality industry including:
  - Food and Beverage
  - Kitchen
  - Front Office
  - Housekeeping
  - Human Resources
  - Sales & Marketing
  - Property Maintenance & Operations
  - Financial Control
  - Small Business
  - Leisure & Entertainment
  - Gaming

Element 1
Develop mission statements

Performance Criteria
- Mission statements developed reflect nature of operation and are service oriented.
- Staff are involved in development of mission statement.

Element 2
Develop a service oriented organisational culture.

Performance Criteria
- Communication structures appropriate to the development of a service oriented culture are developed.
- Service standards and goals are clearly defined and communicated.

Element 3
Apply service management and quality assurance principles.

Performance Criteria
- Management techniques used at the work level are consistent with service management principles.
- Management techniques used at the work unit level are consistent with quality assurance principles.

Element 4
Measure the quality of service.

Performance Criteria
- Service is measured against established standards.
- Standards relate to the requirements of customers.
- Quantative and qualitative data is evaluated.
- Both internal and external service provision is measured.

Element 5
Develop service to customer expectations.

Performance Criteria
- Using market research into customer preferences, service provision is adjusted in line with research.
- Service is adjusted to meet the expectations of individual guests as requested.

Element 6
Manage quality improvement.

Performance Criteria
- A plan for establishing and maintaining staff involvement in quality improvement is developed.
- Staff are involved in establishing quality standards.
- Staff are involved in monitoring and evaluating quality.
- Staff are involved in on-going quality improvement.

Evidence Guide
- Evidence of knowledge and understanding of the following is required:
  - Theory of Service Management
  - Theory of TQM—service organisations

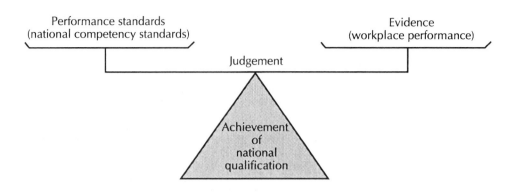

Figure 11.2   Performance appraisal using a competency-based system

As can be seen, the management unit 'Develop and Maintain Service Quality' has six elements, and each of these elements have their associated performance criteria. The element therefore refers to what has to be done, and the performance criteria to how well it must be done. The range of variables statement describes the context or conditions in which the performance occurs.

In assessing competence, evidence has to be accumulated in relation to these units/elements and this is then weighed against the performance criteria. If the evidence meets the performance criteria the individual has achieved competency in the unit, but if the evidence fails to meet the criteria, the individual must spend more time collecting further evidence (that is, more detailed or more relevant evidence).

Before going any further, it must be pointed out that industry standards are not the only standards: there are also cross-industry standards and enterprise standards. The National Training Board (1992) describes these as follows:

> *Industry standards* are national competency standards endorsed for a specific industry. They are the focal category of standards.
>
> *Cross-industry standards* are based on competencies common to a range of industries. They facilitate portability, consistency and efficiency in standards development.
>
> *Enterprise standards* consist of competencies developed and used specifically at enterprise level.

Reviewing these standards in reverse order, *enterprise standards* are developed for individual organisations and businesses and are geared towards the way in which the organisation operates. For example, an organisation may take and develop in more detail the industry

STAN, of Chippendale, this week ordered a mushroom pizza to be delivered but instead received a seafood pizza. He rang the shop. "We can have someone out in half an hour with a replacement," Stan was told, "but if you don't want that, put the seafood one in your freezer and we'll be out to swap it next time we're near you."

(*SMH*, 1/7/94)

It's Mac Time

McDonald's Australia has long been recognised for its commitment to practical, on-the-job training and for the skills that its employees develop during their time with the company. As the company's Managing Director, Mr Charlie Bell points out, "I often meet people who tell me they began their working life with McDonald's and other employers, from a wide range of industries constantly tell me how some of their best people are the ones with McDonald's training behind them.

It is therefore exciting that this company has now joined the ranks of so many others in Australian industry who have embraced the tenants of the National Training Reform Agenda and have developed national competencies for their crew operations.

More exciting still is the fact that McDonald's are the first enterprise to have been recognised as an enterprise CSB. Their standards have been endorsed by the National Training Board and aligned to the Australian Standards Framework at levels 1-2.

Recently McDonald's pilot Australian Vocational Certificate (AVC) was launched by the Commonwealth Minister for Schools, Vocational Education and Training, Ross Free. At the launch Mr Bell reinforced, "it goes without saying that training is a top priority for McDonald's and the results of the company's commitment are shown every time a customer goes into one of our stores and gets cheerful, efficient service and has an order handled with courtesy and speed."

Ms Deanne Bevan, National Employee Relations Manager for McDonald's, went on to explain, "McDonald's is delighted to be able to offer our young crew formal, nationally recognised qualifications based on our endorsed standards for the training they undertake with us because this formal recognition will enable them to develop their career paths and make the most of job opportunities throughout their working lives." Mr Bell was also quick to point out that, "by next year McDonald's will have over 40,000 crew employees Australia wide and although this program is a pilot, the company hopes that these developments will eventually enable us to offer nationally recognised training to all these workers."

"In developing our standards" Ms Bevan commented, "we used the expertise of a consultant and gained valuable advice from the National Training Board". During this process we also consulted with the Retail and Hospitality CSB's regarding the relationship between our standards and existing endorsed industry standards as well as reviewing, as appropriate, existing cross-industry standards."

Deanne went on to say that, "the next step is the development of our AVC curriculum and training materials based on our National Training Board endorsed standards".

[NTB Network, National Training Board, No. 13 (April) 1994, p. 1]

standard to suit the style and methods adopted by their specific enterprises. An example is shown in the article from the National Training Board's newsletter, where company-specific standards have been developed for McDonald's Australia (in this case using national standards for the hospitality and retail industries) to form the basis for its competency-based training programs.

Cross-industry standards include competencies such as communications, which when achieved, can be transported by individuals from one industry to another. Many vocational training courses include cross-industry competencies (for example, team-building), and the advantage for the candidates is that they are automatically exempt from similar modules in other courses. Previously, if one studied retailing in one state and travelled to another to study hospitality, the inter-state college would not recognise the communications component. Since being defined, these cross-industry competencies are now portable from industry to industry and college to college.

Industry standards are endorsed by industry bodies for the whole of that industry. They are expressed in broad terms so that they are appropriate for a range of organisations. For example, in the hospitality industry, the service quality unit of competency reproduced in this chapter could be used for assessment of managers in pubs, hotels, clubs and restaurants. The benefits for individuals working in any of these areas is that their industry-based competencies are portable within the industry and within the vocational training sector. Competency in a given unit can be achieved by completing competency-based training in a college or in an organisation offering it as in-house training and assessment. Workplace assessments (by licensed assessors) enable candidates to complete units or modules, and these are recognised by training colleges in the same way that achievement of a competency-based module from a college is recognised in the workplace. Individuals who have extensive industry knowledge can also seek formal recognition of their competencies through assessment programs without having to undertake training.

Achievement of competency is thus possible through:

- the vocational training sector (public and private providers of competency-based training and assessment);
- in-house training and assessments (competency-based);
- recognition of prior learning—assessment without training.

The outcome in all cases is the achievement of competency in relation to the same industry standards. This ensures that employees in the retail industry, for example, can achieve competency in one unit in one state with one employer, another in another state with another employer, and a range of units in a TAFE college. The value of portability to the individual is clear.

BENEFITS FOR THE INDIVIDUAL AND THE ORGANISATION

From the organisation's viewpoint, the competency-based training and assessment system is a way to formalise training and performance appraisal across an industry. From the country's viewpoint, the aim is increased productivity resulting from training reform and award restructuring. Where competency standards are introduced as part of industrial awards and agreements, these standards are typically built in to the position requirements.

When job specifications were discussed in chapter four, they were used to decide the experience, training, knowledge, skills and other attributes necessary for success in the job. With the introduction of national competency standards, employees are increasingly being considered on the basis of their achievement of units of competency. Being industry-endorsed with specific performance criteria, these units of competency are invaluable to the employer as a basis for understanding in specific terms what the potential employee has to offer.

As competency standards are very explicit (although not to the extent that they are prescriptive), they have a number of advantages. First, the individual receives certification of having achieved competency in a unit. And because the unit's elements and performance criteria are comprehensive, this certification becomes currency for the individual concerned, understood by the entire industry and providers of vocational education and training. It is highly portable, and can be used to describe performance, so that an individual taking a competency certification to new employment can achieve immediate recognition for their achievements. This is increasingly possible between countries where competency standards have been implemented. Even where standards have not, the descriptive nature of the certification is valuable.

Second, by reaching performance criteria, individuals can demonstrate the quality of their performance. For this reason, judgement of evidence of service competence needs to be holistic and integrated (as discussed in chapter nine).

Third, formal recognition of competency can be used as the basis for career progression, including industrial awards and agreements (providing that employees have ready access to assessment).

Finally, assessment in the context of competency-based training is a systematic form of performance appraisal. However, unlike systems used in the past, expectations are explicit and public, and formal certification can be achieved by the individual. This enables the individual to attain promotions and transfers (or even alternative employment) as a direct result of participation in a national effort towards training reform.

COMPETENCY-BASED TRAINING

A competency-based training approach has the following features.

- It focuses on outcomes, on what the trainee can do. The trainee utilises a range of knowledge, skills etc. in producing the outcome. Knowledge, skill and attitude are implicit in the performance.
- It is broad-based, enabling adaptation to the needs of individual enterprises, while at the same time achieving consistency across enterprises and allowing portability for the individual achieving competency.

Figure 11.3 illustrates the assessment process in competency-based training. Assessment can occur as part of in-house or company training; or as recognition of prior learning. Two industry examples of competency-based training are described below.

Industry examples

Hospitality industry

The ACCESS program has been successfully implemented in all Australian states and territories, with 2,074 candidates registered in 1994. It is the outcome of close links between industry and training providers. It has proved to be to their mutual benefit and also to the benefit of candidates, both in the workplace and in training.

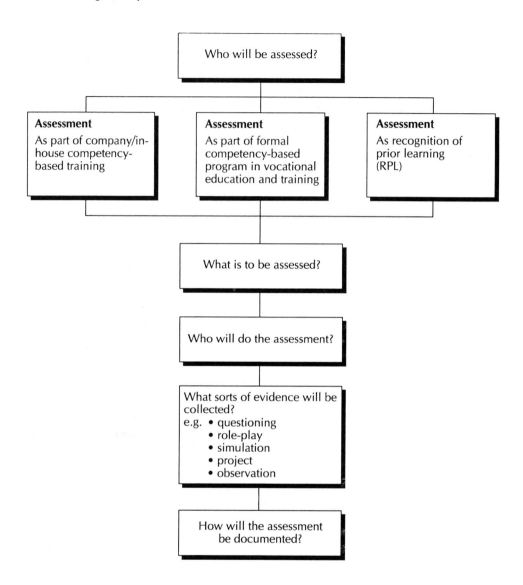

Figure 11.3 Competency-based assessment

In the hospitality industry, skills recognition is built into the award system in hotels, restaurants and clubs. For each position described in the award (or in an enterprise agreement), prerequisite training is specified and this is based on the national competencies developed for the industry. During the implementation phase, employees who were unable to be assessed were 'deemed' as being trained and competent for their level of employment. It is envisaged that, in future, competency-based training and assessment will form the basis for career development and personal achievement. This is a powerful incentive to staff, ensuring the maintenance of quality service as part of a systematic and thorough appraisal process. In linking performance assessment with career development through attainment of nationally recognised certification, this system is far superior to appraisal processes of the past, which were sometimes vague and subjective and did not clearly link to career development.

Australian Nursing Council
The competency standards developed by the Australian Nursing Council cover the full scope of practice of a trained nurse. The feature of interest here is the application of descriptive processes to the assessment of competence.

> The assessment of the ANTRAC competencies cannot be achieved by using a checklist, but relies on tacit knowledge, verbal descriptions and performance criteria. Expert and trained assessors use their tacit knowledge together with assessment guides to achieve a global assessment. This process is much the same as the process of assessment of a fine wine, literature, music or art. Tacit knowledge enables the expert to judge quality.
> (Gonczi, Hager & Athanasou 1993, p. 89)

Of the two dimensions of service described in the first chapter, the procedural dimension lends itself to checklists; the personal dimension does not. And, of course, they cannot be separated. In the end, assessment should be based on the judgement of professionals. Competency standards can formalise this process, assist in the gathering of evidence, by providing guidelines. However, where complex and adaptive behaviours are involved, descriptive processes can prove to be more productive than checklists. Nurses have both aspects of service as part of their duties: procedures upon which lives depend; and personal conduct, to assist the healing process by providing a personal service to each and every patient depending on their needs, both physical and psychological. The two aspects cannot be separated. The nurse communicates while following procedures, just as other service personnel do in other industries.

In their research into assessment system design, Toop, Gibb and Worsnop (1994, p. 87) describe the approach taken in the nursing profession, which has important implications for all service providers who plan to use competency-based training and assessment:

> A key element of the new assessment technology is the recognition that nursing involves applying skills and knowledge to a multitude of different contexts and that setting a relationship with a client is fundamental to the competencies. There is, therefore, a three way relationship between nurse, client and the context in which the nurse is working and it is this whole scenario which includes knowledge, attitudes and skills that has to be considered by the assessor when a judgement is being made about a nurse's

performance. The assessment of competence must therefore take into account the nurse and client in a particular situation.

In all service industries, therefore,

ASSESSMENT OF COMPETENCE MUST TAKE INTO ACCOUNT THE SERVICE PROVIDER (STAFF MEMBER) AND THE CUSTOMER IN A **PARTICULAR** SITUATION.

This brings into focus an aspect of the model for quality service (Figures 1.2, 8.1, 9.1 and 10.1) previously alluded to but not discussed in detail. This is the *context* in which the performance takes place. Service personnel adapt their behaviours to different contexts. Some contexts were discussed earlier, such as the importance of the situation, the speed with which the activity would need to be completed etc. In the nursing example, one can clearly imagine the contexts in which procedure would dominate over anything else. In all service, the staff member has to decide how much time is available to assist, advise, discuss and to chat about unrelated matters.

Offering service (and we do this every day in one way or another to others all around) entails high-level performance, requiring spontaneous evaluation of a multitude of factors. Thus, is assessment of performance difficult, if not impossible? Of course not: judges of performances on the ice rink, in the show ring and on the football field have no difficulty if they are experts in their field.

Research currently being carried out (Gonczi, Palmer & Hager 1994) suggests that experts have no difficulty in rating performance as unsatisfactory, satisfactory or highly satisfactory. For experts, these rating judgements are based on experience gained in the field or industry. Their judgements can be assisted by discussions relating to benchmarks for the performance levels. It is therefore possible to grade performance on a criterion. Wolf (1993) has suggested that people operate with complex, holistic, tacit models of performance on which they base their judgements. A global evaluation, nonetheless, still needs to be enlarged upon by descriptive feedback.

EXERCISES AND DISCUSSION

1. What are the benefits of competency-based assessment and training for an organisation?

2. What are the benefits of competency-based assessment and training for the individuals in this organisation?

3. Assessment of competence involves collecting evidence to demonstrate competence. In the area of customer service, what sort of evidence would be appropriate for trainees in colleges? And for those in workplaces?

4. Small business is generally the last to get involved in major projects of this nature. If you were running a small business, what would your views be on competency-based training and assessment?

5. Review the following terms in the glossary and define them in your own words:

    Appraisal
    Assessment
    Competency
    Criterion-referenced assessment
    Holistic assessment
    Recognition of prior learning
    Reliability
    Validity

6. Every effort should be made to ensure reliability (repeatability) and validity (measuring what is intended) in the assessment process. Is this problematic in competency-based assessment of service ability?

12

MANAGING FOR CHANGE: continuous quality improvement

SUMMARY

This chapter introduces a strategy for continuous quality improvement in service through ongoing training which is learner-focused. Since front-line staff are usually one of the best sources of information about customer needs, their input in the process of change is most important, particularly as it impacts on customers. Being proactive is the name of the game in the service industry. To achieve this, a creative, learning culture is necessary. Staff need to learn how to learn, and to learn to adapt quickly to changing customer expectations.

CHAPTER OBJECTIVES

On completion of this chapter you will be able to:

- identify training situations in which high levels of participation are desirable;
- describe the stages for achieving valued outcomes, following Egan's model;
- implement the process in training focused on improving customer service;
- evaluate the success of the process used for this learner-directed learning.

MANAGING FOR CHANGE: CONTINUOUS QUALITY IMPROVEMENT

In order to maintain and improve on the quality of service and ensure customer satisfaction, ongoing staff training and career development are necessary. In the past, training has most often been in the form of short, formal sessions that bear little or no resemblance to circumstances in the workplace. Being highly theoretical or overly simplistic, much training fails to interest employees at all. Even where it is enjoyable (most feedback sheets measure this and not learning) and relevant, it is often argued that the impact of the training is minimal and that no measurable changes occur in performance. The following steps are suggested for ongoing training, for continuous quality improvement and for high levels of employee commitment to a culture of life-long learning.

STRATEGY FOR DISCUSSION RELATING TO LEARNING OUTCOMES

The strategy for learning-related discussion herein presented is based on Egan (1988b). Egan's model (Figure 12.1) for managing change is devised for application to any organisation, and here the specific application of the model is to negotiating

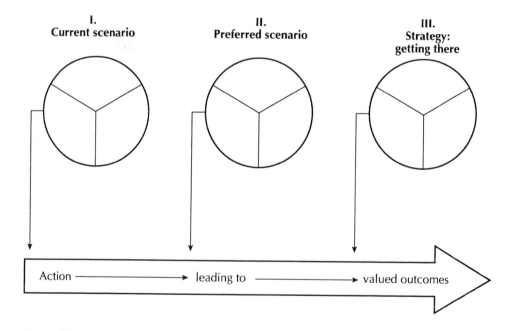

Figure 12.1 A model for organisation change
(Reproduced from *Change Agent Skills B: Managing Innovation and Change* by G. Egan. Copyright © 1988 by Pfieffer & Company. Used with permission.)

IT WAS going to be one of those romantic evenings to be treasured for a lifetime. Michael Levy, of Vaucluse, took Lynette Carvalho to an intimate dinner at a self-styled "exclusive" restaurant in the Blue Mountains, at which he planned to propose. They ordered an expensive bottle of red, got their garlic bread, decided against an entree because they weren't over-hungry—then sat waiting for 70 minutes for the main course, filet mignon.

It never came—the somewhat ruffled waitress told them that "the chef has had a bad day and is upset that you haven't ordered an entree, and refuses to cook your main meal". They left, the engagement ring still in Michael's pocket. Fortunately, the Fairmont, where they were staying, provided a good enough ambience for the "Will you? — Yes indeed".

(SMH, 6/9/94)

learning outcomes and the means of achieving them in the workplace.

Reasons for change

Learning is often a response to a need, a creative response to the environment. An individual perceives that the acquisition of skills, knowledge and other abilities will enable him or her to better cope with a changing and complex environment. In the case of quality service, the changing environment generally relates to changes in customer needs and wants, and to a need to continually upgrade products and services. As part of the learning process, the emphasis on change is a valuable first step towards defining goals for learning.

Where the individual (or the team) is able to define where they are now and where they would like to be (or should be), the gap between the two forms the basis for developing a strategy to attain this goal. Vroom's (1964) expectancy theory describes goals as having a 'valence' (that is, a perceived value). Where the individual sees their desired goal as having a high valence and as being attainable, the motivation to reach that goal is high. This 'expectancy' is a perceptual factor, directly related to the individual's level of motivation. It is determined by the individual's perception that the goal has value, is achievable and reasonable (that is, it is a 'valued outcome').

One way in which individuals are allowed to set their own goals or agendas for learning is through the use of the learning contract (Knowles 1984). Learning contracts can be developed individually or on a group basis, and as such, can form the basis for the development of highly cohesive work teams. Alternatively, participation in competency-based training (with standards defined in terms of meeting customer needs for quality service) is another avenue for achieving quality assurance in customer service and (the underlying goal of) career development for the individual.

The strategy suggested here for planning learning outcomes aims to accomplish two things. First, to provide a step-by-step approach for discussing the learning process and outcomes, in order to maximise learning. Second, to provide the opportunity to modify the training methods and assessment requirements on either a group or individual basis. The strategy can, therefore, be used on a one-to-one basis or used to provide the foundation for team discussion or negotiation.

It may well be that the trainees agree that the learning outcomes defined by the manager or trainer are valuable and realistic. This may result from the persuasive efforts of the trainer. The point, however, is that the trainee(s) and instructor have

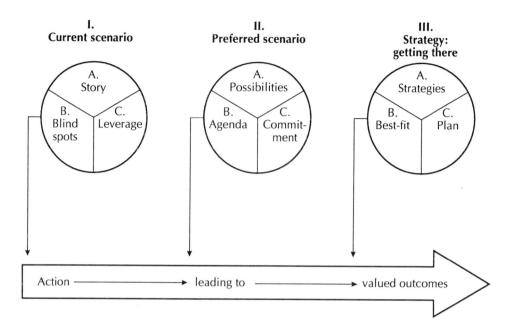

Figure 12.2 A model for organisation change (Egan, 1988)
(Reproduced from *Change Agent Skills B: Managing Innovation and Change* by G. Egan.
Copyright © 1988 by Pfieffer & Company. Used with permission.)

reached a consensus, where the outcomes are explicit and the methods used to reach them are agreed. We could go further to suggest that the choice of didactic instruction (that is, one-way training) should occur only when the issues of goals, content and teaching and learning methods have been discussed. Where competency-based instruction is envisaged, the learning outcomes may be decided in terms of modules, elements and standards. Moreover, the individuals themselves may wish to decide on the way in which these standards are achieved. Whatever the outcomes and means to achieve those outcomes, there are some three steps recommended for the development of training that is needs-based and relevant to the achievement of quality service.

The steps that follow are based on those suggested by Egan (1988b), modified to suit a formal learning context. They are presented graphically in Figure 12.2.

Step I

Stage a—The current scenario
Egan refers to stage Ia as 'telling the story'. In discussion with employees, the aims are to explore previous learning experiences (to find out about preferred learning styles) and to explore practical experience in the field (which could be brought to bear during the learning process). Lindeman (1926), in his famous essays on adult education, talks about adults who learn through confronting experience, 'who dig down into the reservoirs of their experience before resorting to texts and

secondary facts' (1926, p. 11). Thus, this is a critical first step; without fully exploring the needs, interests and experiences of learners the trainer is likely to make many assumptions about the 'best fit' in terms of instructional strategies.

Questions appropriate at this stage:
Can you describe a learning experience about which you felt quite positive?
Can you describe a negative experience in an educational setting?
Can you describe some of the incidents that led you to be here today?
Why did you decide to embark on this training program?
Are there special issues you would like addressed?
Do you have any particular interest areas?
How much experience do you have in this field?
What would you like to achieve in doing this training program?

Stage b—Challenging blind spots and developing new perspectives

Efforts to raise the individuals' level of awareness are part of what arguably is the most important phase in the early stages of teaching and learning. Egan refers to this process as:

> seeing things more clearly, getting the picture, getting insights, developing new perspective, spelling out implications, perception transformation, developing new frames of reference, looking for meaning, perception shifting, seeing the bigger picture, frame breaking, developing different angles, seeing things in context, rethinking, getting a more objective view interpreting, overcoming blind spots, analysing, second-level learning, double-loop learning, reframing, thinking creatively, reconceptualising, discovery, have an 'ah-ha' experience, developing a new outlook ...
>
> (Egan 1988b, p. 37)

In the early stages of any learning, the individual needs to form an overall picture of the area of study. In most cases, this perspective involves listing the topics or discussing the competency unit to be covered. Very often the trainer describes the importance of each topic and is persuasive in describing the potential value of the outcomes to staff. Descriptions of personal experiences, industry issues and/or accomplishments of previous employees are used to endorse the general aims of the course. But this can be done without challenging the employee's current thinking whatsoever. By introducing novel information, different perspectives or creative and critical approaches to the subject area, higher levels of interest and motivation can be engendered in the individual.

Next, this interest must be taken and turned into a learning experience that is valuable to the individual. It must be directed; it is more than just a heightened awareness. It must lead to action. The foci are on action and outcome (individual, with personal relevance, and group). Frequently outcomes are described as being beneficial to the reputation of the organisation. This should be a secondary outcome for the employee or the team. The learning should *first* meet their needs.

Questions appropriate at this stage:
What are the problems that need to be addressed in service delivery?
What are the problems that you have in this area?
What are the assumptions underlying the problems and how can we challenge them?
What are the opportunities for you individually and as a group in this area?
Are there barriers that prevent you and/or the group from seeing the opportunities objectively?
How would you define success in the area of quality service, and what would it lead to for you and/or the group?

Exploration of differing perspectives should assist in developing foci on the individual and his or her ownership of the problem, the opportunities for resolution, and the need for personal action in order to reach personal goals.

Stage c—Leverage: the search for high-impact problems and opportunities

The brainstorming process used at the previous stage could lead to a wide range of problems and opportunities. Decisions now need to be made about which of these problems and opportunities are most suitable for consideration during the training program. Leverage refers to the selection of points of influence, but note that the action outcomes resulting from this must be productive in terms of time and effort. In other words, goals or outcomes need to be realistic and achievable.

This process is aimed at choosing high priority problems and eliminating those that cannot be achieved realistically by the individual or group in training. Where the issue requires group activity to achieve successful outcomes, productivity is an important consideration. Team approaches, although they have numerous benefits, are also time-consuming, requiring high levels of participation and commitment. For both team and individual training, organisational constraints, resource limitations and the time available both inside and outside the training room all need to be considered in selecting learning goals.

The outcomes selected must be clearly defined and action-oriented.

Questions appropriate at this stage:
Which of the problems raised cannot be realistically tackled in this training program?
Which of the problems can be eliminated from discussion?
Which of the problems and opportunities are the highest priorities?
Which of these opportunities are under the control of the trainees in terms of potential outcomes?
What are the constraints of the training program?
Are the resulting learning goals achievable within the constraints of the training program?

Step II

Stage a—Developing a range of possible futures

Egan (1988b) distinguishes between solutions that are in essence actions that need to be taken and 'what will be in place' once the solutions are implemented. The latter looks beyond steps, stages and strategies to a vision of the future (or a 'preferred scenario'), with the goals or outcomes having been achieved. The visualisation of this can further contribute to employee motivation and commitment to the chosen outcomes.

Questions appropriate at this stage:
How will the future look when I/we have achieved the outcomes?
Where could this lead?

Stage b—Turning the scenario into a viable agenda

Egan offers the following criteria for developing a viable agenda for the preferred scenario.

1. Stated as accomplishments or outcomes, rather than means or strategies.
2. Clear and specific.
3. Measurable or verifiable.
4. Realistic.
5. Substantive (or at least adequate).
6. In keeping with the overall strategy and values.
7. Set in a reasonable time frame.

Questions appropriate at this stage:
Which of the outcomes have the highest priority personally and collectively?
Are the outcomes selected really outcomes or just strategies?
Can these outcomes be measured or verified in some way?
Can these outcomes be achieved realistically within the available time frame?

Stage c—Commitment: linking the agenda to action

Commitment to course outcomes is not automatic. Nor are the persuasive efforts of the instructor adequate in selling the outcomes as favourable. Real change requires a personal commitment on the part of participating trainees. As Egan (1988b) points out, it requires a search for incentives that make sense for these people, in this situation, at this time, with respect to this agenda and under these conditions. The all-important perception on the part of the individual is that these outcomes have a high value, are realistic and personally achievable.

Step III

Stage a—Strategies for getting there

The means of achieving outcomes are often varied, and the most efficient and effective of these need to be defined. Egan suggests that the creative person is characterised by an 'acceptance of ambiguity and flexibility', 'tolerance for complexity', and independence. Creativity is 'hindered by such things as fear, fixed habits, dependence on authority and perfectionism' (Egan 1988b, p. 101). Adult learners who are highly dependent need to be encouraged to develop more autonomy. Where flexibility is introduced into program processes and outcomes, the trainer cannot afford to have a full class of dependent trainees. Self-directedness should be the aim of adult education. However, trainers cannot be unrealistic in their expectations for self-directedness: trainees accustomed to didactic training would find themselves floundering and would become rapidly frustrated. This is why the exploration of previous learning experiences in step I was vital.

At this stage, a brainstorming of strategies is recommended, with the trainer's initial acceptance of all suggestions (including the most unusual). Criticism or evaluation of suggested strategy should not occur until the next stage. A key point here is that trainees are seldom aware of the range of outcomes and possible training and learning methods that can be adopted. Very often the trainer decides, on behalf of the trainees, what will be appropriate for them (an analogy is the poor pooch whose owner makes decisions about the kind of food he will enjoy). Although often unable to identify the alternatives explicitly, most trainees are quite capable of stating their preferences given range of choices.

Stage b—Choosing strategies

Egan (1988b, pp. 110–14) suggests the following in the selection of a strategy to achieve the preferred scenario:

- Choose a strategy or a set of strategies from a pool of strategies.
- Make sure that strategies are clear and specific.
- Link the strategy to the preferred outcome.
- Choose realistic strategies.
- Set strategies in a reasonable time frame.
- Choose strategies that contribute substantially to outcomes.
- Make sure that the players own the strategies.
- Keep the strategies in line with organizational values and with the values of those charged with implementing them.

This last point is most important. Managers and trainers are accountable for the outcomes of the learning process. This process of choosing strategies to be documented and finally agreed by all parties.

Stage c—Formulating plans

Individual performance plans need to be devised for each employee (or team, if working collectively). These plans need formal agreement and commitment. Sub-goals and sub-strategies need to be devised for implementation within a suitable time frame during the program, and must be realistic. Progress needs to be appraised regularly.

THE TRANSITION

Effective leadership by the trainer/manager to ensure that plans are implemented and outcomes achieved is vital.

> Effective leaders not only turn visions into realistic agendas and arouse enthusiasm for these agendas by the very way in which they communicate them to others, but they also create a ferment of problem solving and learning around these agendas and make sure that actors persist until the agendas are accomplished. In many ways the transition phase is about tactics and logistics. Tactics is the art of being able to adapt a plan to the immediate situation; it is the art of persistence. This includes being able to change the plan on the spot in order to handle unforeseen complications. Logistics is the art of being able to provide the resources needed for the implementation of any given plan when they are required. (Egan 1988b, p. 131)

Encouragement, direction, challenge and support are some of the approaches that could be required in monitoring and assisting employees in their progress towards goals. Flexible styles of leadership based on situational and individual factors are called for. This is the real challenge for supervisors and managers. Can they create an environment in which people learn, in which staff are self-directed and autonomous, and in which employees achieve goals which have personal value?

EXERCISES AND DISCUSSION

1. Describe the type of training for which you would use the approach suggested in this chapter.

2. Using the stages of Egan's model and the suggested questions, develop your own training program. Choose valued outcomes for improving your own customer service competency, and work through the questions to develop plans, implement and evaluate them.

3. Use the same model and process to develop a group training exercise in the area of continuous quality improvement for customer service.

4. Contrast the two processes, individual and group, and evaluate them in terms of training effectiveness.

13

DISCIPLINE AND DISMISSAL

SUMMARY

This chapter deals with the topic of dismissal (an appropriate topic for chapter thirteen). Good selection and training, as well as preventative measures such as performance feedback, should reduce the likelihood of dismissal. However, where it does become necessary, a dismissal policy should have certain features. These are described in this chapter.

CHAPTER OBJECTIVES

On completion of this chapter you will be able to:

- explain how preventative measures can reduce the likelihood of dismissal;
- develop a disciplinary policy;
- write a warning letter;
- fully document employment, training, performance appraisal and dismissal processes.

DISCIPLINE AND DISMISSAL

Staff who are not competent in certain ares are a burden to an organisation and can cause immense damage to its reputation. Having implemented good recruitment and selection, ensured that all employees participate in induction sessions and that all are trained to perform competently, there should be no need for dismissal procedures. Unfortunately there is the occasional employee who does not perform to standard, and to whom no amount of counselling or training seems to make a difference.

Four considerations are important here prior to taking any disciplinary action:

- Is the employee damaging the organisation's reputation of good service to its external customers?
- Is the employee proving poor internal service to other employees and departments?
- Is there a risk to the health and safety of other staff when this employee fails to follow instructions?
- Is there a risk that this employee will cause litigation to be brought against the organisation by a member of the public as a result of the employee's action or negligence?

Managers fearful of unfair dismissal claims are often loath to dismiss incompetent staff. They forget that the law places a burden on them to manage effectively and to meet minimum standards. Management is vicariously liable for the actions of employees, so that any action or negligence on the part of staff members rests squarely at the feet of management. It is not the employee, but the organisation and its representatives who then face court action.

It is becoming increasingly important that managers are able to demonstrate in writing the reasons for an employee's dismissal. General guidelines for handling performance problems, ensuring that all parties are fully informed and providing opportunities for appeal, are now explained.

GENERAL GUIDELINES

Dismissing employees is the ultimate act of 'punishment' a manager can take. No-one likes dismissing people from their jobs—in one way it is an admission that the manager made a wrong decision in the first instance. It is so much better to avert dismissal by taking all appropriate care right from the start.

Selection

Managers have a responsibility to ensure that staff work in a competent manner (a legal and an ethical issue). The clear starting point to ensure that this is the case is the selection of competent staff.

Guidelines presented earlier in this book for employing competent staff included the development of a job description and job specification. The job description listed the tasks and procedures to be followed by an employee. As such, it provides a solid foundation for issuing a reprimand: the employee has previously been fully informed of their duties and has been issued with company procedure guidelines. The development of a job specification enables the manager to list the attributes an individual should have in order to perform the duties listed in the job description. Where there is no match between the individual and the job specification, the person being employed is clearly not competent and managers would then need to show how this training need was addressed.

It is also possible that the gap between expectations and performance is caused by the employee claiming to have skills which they did not. This is sometimes the case in the computer field which, being highly technical, does not allow for simple appraisal of the individual's level of expertise. Very careful reference checking is then essential to validate the individual's claims. Skills tests, such as those mentioned in earlier chapters, are another method for improving the validity of selection decisions. Conducted in simulated work environments, such tests need not take long and could be a far more accurate way of validating an individual's claims to experience and ability. (Nonetheless, it is always questionable whether the interview is the most appropriate method for selection of employees.)

DINING OUT news from Dungog: a letter in the *Bellingen Courier* passes on a complaint from a Victorian visitor who ordered seafood at a local eating place. He felt the fish tasted odd so he sent it back to the kitchen and asked for another dish. Said the letter: "The irritable and most unfriendly chef promptly returned with the rejected fish and upon slamming it down on the table expressed her belief that the fish was fine and suggested firmly that he Eat It! In disgust and disbelief, the customer placed his meal on the cash counter and turned to go. [As he] walked out of the restaurant, he felt a considerable thud as the remains of the fish splattered across the floor, table and chairs and all over his back! Perhaps he didn't realise the chef's specialty was 'Seafood and Duck'." Or flying fish. (SMH, 23/6/94)

'They asked me if I had worked in a bar before. I hadn't, but I knew I would learn fast, so I said yes. I soon found out that pulling beer was a lot harder than I realised. I often had more head than beer or more beer in the trough than in the glass. It took hours before I got it right, but fortunately my new supervisor was patient with me, and the customers thought it was quite a laugh.'

It might not be quite so amusing if this new employee had breached legal guidelines for, say, serving under-age drinkers and incurred penalties for the company and risked its licence. A simple skills test or a few questions in an interview could avoid any such débâcle.

In summary, the selection process can bring about two possibilities: first, the employment of an individual who is competent to perform the duties (this having been checked by validating all information and recording this process in writing). Alternatively, it may be that the individual being employed will require training. This training need will be taken into account if dismissal does occurs and it is claimed that such action is 'wrongful'. It is unfair or wrongful if nothing was done to remedy the gap between the needs of the position and the employee's skill or knowledge, knowing such a gap existed.

Induction

The importance of careful and thorough employee induction cannot be stressed enough. In addition to reinforcing the organisation's service culture through explanations of mission, strategic plan, marketing efforts and the like, the induction process should ensure that the employee is fully aware of all legal responsibilities towards customers and towards the health and safety of other employees. All topics covered in the induction session and in later explanations should be issued to the employee in writing in the form of an employee handbook, and the employee should sign an acknowledgement of having read and understood rules, policies and guidelines. This signature ensures that there is, on file, written documentation of the organisation's efforts to properly advise the employee of its expectations.

Training

Training needs, resulting from the selection and employment of inexperienced individuals, or the development of new procedures and products, need to be met by formal training programs. All training, whether on a one-to-one basis or part of team training, should be recorded and formalised. Where the industry has defined competency standards, supervisors and managers can use these as the basis training and development. Where the employee has attempted a training module and has not achieved competence, this needs to be recorded on their personal file as further documentation to assist in the case of a claim for unfair dismissal.

Thus, prior to any disciplinary action, the manager will already have a substantial paper trail to substantiate the organisation's commitment to make clear its expectations of its staff.

DISCIPLINARY PROCEDURES

Assuming that all the policies and procedures for hiring and training staff are consistently applied, it is still possible that performance problems emerge. In the above example of the inexperienced employee behind the bar, the performance problem could be a failure to check the identification of under-age drinkers. This could result from the employee's laziness, or from their attempts to increase tips and revenue by increasing patronage (relying on the word spreading). If this is so, a warning, the beginning of an organisation's disciplinary procedure, is necessary—though where sound employment practices are in place, warnings are seldom necessary.

When having to apply disciplinary procedures, managers must ensured that all staff are treated consistently. It is not acceptable for management to turn a blind eye in some instances while taking action in others. Moral and ethical responsibilities towards employees are just as important as legal responsibilities. For example, drinking on duty is often sanctioned in the hospitality trade, but employers who do this are on fragile ground when taking action for drunkenness on duty. Furthermore, health and safety risks are high where this sanction occurs.

Prompt action is another factor to be considered here. Timing is all important in disciplining wayward employees. A serious breach of conduct needs to be raised and dealt with immediately. The following example warrants immediate action, regardless of the convenience or profitability of delaying action.

'The apprentice deliberately placed the soup ladle on the grill, and then using a cloth, put it beside the soup tureen. He then told the chef that the customer was waiting for the soup order. Despite his hand being badly burned in this incident, the chef did not take disciplinary action. He waited until after the busy Christmas period to do something about it.'

First warning

The first warning should be a mild discussion. It may be that the employee was quite unaware of the deficiency, and if not handled carefully they could become quite demotivated. The words 'problem' and 'warning' should thus be avoided if this is the case.

The following points should be raised in the discussion between the manager and employee.

- Describe the action or negligence that has occurred.
- Explain why this was not satisfactory.
- Ask why this happened.
- Explain what is necessary for reaching the organisation's required standards.
- Set a review time to look at the matter again.
- Remind the employee of their importance and value.

The description of performance expectations should always be phrased in positive terms. Often managers will say 'Don't be so rude to customers' when they should be explaining and showing the employee what good, polite service looks like. Sometimes the employee has no idea what he or she is doing wrong and no conception of what positive expectations entail. A training session on the personal dimension of service may rectify any shortcomings. In any case, a diary note of the first warning should be made.

'George, I have noticed that, when working behind the bar, you have not asked some very young-looking customers to show you their identification. There are two youngsters sitting over there that you have just served. Why didn't you ask to see identification? As you know, the penalties for serving under-age drinkers are severe—not only are the fines very high, but we also risk losing our liquor licence. If we lose our licence we close down.

'Please make sure that you check the identification of every customer who looks like they might be under-age. If you like, we can spend some time together on a busy night and see how accurate both our assessments of age are by checking a few of the younger-looking ones. I would like to talk to you about this again next Wednesday, and would like to be sure that you are following the procedures.

'I know that this is difficult thing to do when you are busy. Our sales revenue has gone up in the past month, and this is a result of your effort to speed up service. At the same time, it is important that we meet our legal obligations.'

Written warning

If, following the first warning, an employee has not changed or corrected their performance, a second warning should be given, this time in writing. It should include the following points.

- The date and details of the first verbal warning.
- The performance that is unsatisfactory and why.
- The steps required to remedy the situation.
- Date and time of the next review.
- A statement to the effect that a failure to rectify the situation will lead to dismissal.
- A statement that the letter will be kept on the employee's file.

SAMPLE LETTER—First written warning

Dear Joan,

I must bring to your attention that you have been leaving the sales counter without authorisation for extended periods. This matter was raised in a verbal discussion on 15th June, and I wish to bring it again to your attention. When you leave your counter for lengthy periods, as you did this morning without telling your supervisor, customers are kept waiting for long periods and there is nobody to answer the phone. This morning it took us fifteen minutes to track you down. If you do need to leave your area for more than five minutes you must advise your supervisor so that someone can be found to take your place.

Can I remind you that you have a fifteen-minute coffee break, morning and afternoon, and a one hour lunch break. You are expected to return promptly to take over from the relieving person, otherwise the next person is late for their break. If you need to leave your area at any other time for more than five minutes you must advise your supervisor so that you can be relieved by another member of staff. We cannot keep up our standard of service if counters are unattended.

Failure to remedy this situation could result in dismissal. A copy of this letter will be kept on your personal file. I would like to review this matter on 2nd July at 10 a.m., and hope that at that time I find that further absences have not occurred.

[Signed]
MANAGER   EMPLOYEE   WITNESS (UNION)

- Signature of the employer.
- Signatures of the employee (to acknowledge receipt of the warning letter) and (union) witness if possible.

Final written warning

If an employee still fails to take heed of the verbal and first written warnings, a final written warning should be issued. This is the same as the first written warning, except that it states that a failure to remedy the situation as suggested will result in dismissal on a given date. The warning could be phrased along similar lines as the above sample first written warning.

Summary dismissal

Summary dismissal, that is, instant dismissal without notice, occurs where there is a serious breach of an employment contract, such as a case of theft or drunkenness. This is otherwise known as wilful misconduct. Grounds for summary dismissal should be made known to all employees in their employee handbook. In these serious cases, the series of warnings as described above are inappropriate as the dismissal is immediate.

APPEALS

In any disciplinary procedure, there should also be the inclusion of an appeal process that allows individuals to seek a review of the circumstances surrounding the disciplinary action or dismissal. An appeal allows for resolution of issues before the case escalates and results in industrial or other action. The example that springs to mind is the employee who was found by his supervisor in the pub on a day that he had called in sick. In response to his dismissal, all other workers walked off site, saying that he could do as he pleased on a sick day.

Appeal processes allow for a more thorough review of the facts of the case and consideration of mitigating circumstances.

Disciplinary procedures should ensure that

- prompt action was taken.
- the employee was alerted to the performance deficiency and the possible consequences of not meeting requirements.
- the standards or requirements for competent performance were made clear to the employee.

DINING OUT NOTES: A partner in the country restaurant that saw flying fish on the menu ... has written to the Bellingen *Courier* with his version of the lively meal: "The male visitor was not told to eat the fish as claimed in the letter. He was simply informed on inspection that the trout has a distinctive smell and the meal was to standard. At this point, the visitor threw the fish at the chef in what amounted to an aggravated assault on our lady staff member." The restaurant, he said, has served 15,000 trout meals. "I could take legal action ... and feed some lawyers," he wrote. "Instead, I prefer to feed your readers"—and offered free meals to the first 20 who flourish his letter and order a meal.
(SMH, 25/6/94)

- efforts were made to assist the employee to reach those standards.
- the requirements were reasonable.
- investigations were fair and impartial.
- similar behaviour by other employees has been treated in a consistent manner.
- the employee was fully aware of the organisation's rules and regulations.
- mitigating circumstances have been taken into account.
- the union has been advised and involved where appropriate.
- there has not been any breach of legislation, such anti-discrimination, by the organisation in disciplining an employee.

DISCIPLINARY POLICY

The organisation's disciplinary policy (along with procedures for appeals) should be spelt out in the employee handbook, in clear and simple language. The handbook should explain the types of conduct that will lead to disciplinary action, and the types of conduct that will lead to summary dismissal. Working dangerously, using abusive language, stealing or using mind-altering substances could be examples of conduct leading to summary dismissal.

An example of an organisation's disciplinary policy is given following the exercises. It may be useful as a model.

EXERCISES AND DISCUSSION

1. List the written information you should have on hand to demonstrate that a careful selection decision was made, that the employee was aware of and understood all rules and regulations, that they were adequately trained and received regular performance assessments or feedback, and that warnings were issued where necessary.

2. Write a warning letter to a staff member who has previously been verbally warned about the number of incoming and outgoing personal phone calls.

3. Draft a disciplinary policy for an employee handbook.

EXAMPLE OF DISCIPLINARY POLICY

Purpose and scope

The aim of this policy is to make clear to employees the procedures to be followed where disciplinary action is necessary. The process is aimed at resolving these issues, and at achieving and maintaining company standards. It notes the rights of the individual staff member, of other staff and of the customers we serve. Its aim is to ensure that all staff receive fair and consistent treatment.

Principles

1. Disciplinary action will not be taken against an employee until there has been a full investigation.
2. The employee has the right to full disclosure of information and has the right to reply at any stage in the process.
3. The employee has the right to be accompanied by another staff member or union representative.
4. The employee will not be dismissed without warning or notice except in the case of serious and wilful misconduct.
5. The employee will be told, in positive terms, what the standards and expectations are that need to be achieved.
6. Where training is necessary this will be provided.
7. The employee has the right to appeal at any stage of the process.

The warning process

1.   Verbal warning

The employee will be made aware of the issue through an informal verbal warning, which will explain the infringement and the steps necessary to remedy this. The employee will be asked to explain why this breach of company standards has occurred. A review will be scheduled to reassess the situation within a short period. The manager will make a diary note of this warning.

2.   Written warning

If the employee does not reach the standard explained in the previous interview, the next step is a written warning which will be kept on the employee's file. The issue will again be explained and the improvement required spelt out. This will be signed by the employee, the manager and a third party (who may be chosen by the employee). A review period for resolving the performance problem will be set with a date for a further interview. A copy of the written warning will be kept on file for 12 months, after which time, and following satisfactory performance and conduct, it will be destroyed.

3.   Final written warning

This letter will take the same format as the last, and will be used in the case of serious performance problems where the first written warning is waived. It will contain the same detail as the previous written warning, with the statement that it is a final written warning and failure to comply with expectations will result in dismissal. It will advise of the right of appeal.

4. Dismissal

The date on which employment will terminate is given to the employee in writing.

Appeals

Any employee wishing to appeal against any disciplinary action can do so by applying to the Human Resources Manager within two working days.

Serious and wilful misconduct

The following list provides examples of gross misconduct which will lead to summary dismissal:

Theft, fraud or falsification of records
Fighting or assault
Being under the influence of alcohol or illegal drugs during working hours
Deliberate damage to company property
Serious negligence or failure to abide by company rules
Serious insubordination.

14

STAFF TURNOVER

SUMMARY

This chapter discusses the cost of staff turnover to the organisation—the cost of recruiting, selecting, inducting and training of new staff. This, though, is only half the cost; the rest is the damage done to the organisation through poor service due to understaffing and lack of training.

CHAPTER OBJECTIVES

On completion of this chapter you will be able to:

- list the reasons why staff leave;
- explain why exit interviews are useful for feedback purposes;
- conduct an exit interview;
- calculate the costs of staff turnover, direct and indirect;
- calculate the rate of staff turnover;
- develop strategies to reduce staff turnover.

STAFF TURNOVER

If most managers were told that they could save 10 per cent of their wages budget and increase revenue by a further 10 per cent, they would be desperate to know how. Reducing staff turnover has this effect, particularly in an industry that is very labour intensive. In organisations that experience high staff turnover, a sense of instability and discordance is created among the staff. Informal relationships are unstable, and communication is disrupted, with flow-on effects to all departments. This can lead to immense frustration on the part of longer-serving staff members, who also soon become disgruntled.

The reasons why staff leave usually fall into the following categories:

Voluntary	Changing personal circumstances
	Poor pay
	Poor working conditions
	Lack of training and career development
	Lack of incentives
	Lack of motivation
	Incompetent management
	Personality clashes
	Better offers
Involuntary	Redundancy
	Warnings and dismissal with notice
	Summary dismissal.

EXIT INTERVIEW

The exit interview (for want of a better name) is not a dismissal interview but an interview conducted when *any* employee leaves. When one thinks about the effort that goes into employing someone, one really wonders why as much effort doesn't go into their departure. Though an employee leaving (on good terms) is treated to a staff get-together of some form, there should also be a formal interview, similar to the selection interview, conducted with that person. The purpose of this exit interview is to find out why the person is leaving, to get some feedback on job satisfaction and to get some suggestions on improvements. These suggestions are immensely helpful where they might affect customer service. Suggestions relating to the internal service to other departments is also important here: a lack of co-operation between departments can contribute to dissatisfaction within the organisation.

'It sounds like a little thing, but it drives you crazy. Do you know that you can never find a teaspoon in this place? Have you ever tried to set up a banquet for five hundred people with two hundred and ten teaspoons? They go overnight. Purchasing says that the staff throw them out with the food scraps and that the magnets on the bin lids are not strong enough to catch them. Apparently this hotel used ten thousand teaspoons last year. The real problem is that staff run around from one outlet to another stealing them and hiding them so that they don't run short. And then there are the napkins. Housekeeping is careless in folding them. It makes it impossible to do really fancy folds unless they are starched and folded exactly square after ironing. We've asked them time and again ...'

The staff in banks become frustrated when they run out of forms because children have been scribbling on them. This could be solved with a blackboard, high counters, a play area or something similar. One coffee shop that did a roaring trade acted on the suggestion of a staff member and went out and bought a rocking horse and some wooden toys. The staff were being driven crazy by children running around and it was frightening the childless couples away. The play area resolved this problem. The suggestions that emerged in an exit interview are often minor but have important implications for customers.

Most employees leaving the organisation will offer safe and reasonable reasons for doing so. It is only during the exit interview that other, less obvious reasons become apparent. Some of the things that might be asked are the expectations they had of the job when starting and how the organisation met those expectations. A mismatch may have been the result of poor recruitment, selection or induction. Other probing questions could be asked about working conditions, supervision, relationships with other staff, adequacy of training, equipment and so on.

The nature of the exit interview, occurring as it does when the person is leaving, generally leads to the staff member divulging information that might otherwise never see the light of day. Some of these issues raised could be petty grievances, others tip-offs to major fraud. The exit interview is best conducted by someone slightly removed from the department concerned; in large organisations this is the role of the Human Resources Department. The outcomes of these interviews need to be treated judiciously. If the interviews are seen as a slanging match, department heads become very defensive, arguing that third parties can never understand the pressures of work that lead to complaints. Only where there appears to be a trend towards the same type of dissatisfaction should action be taken.

The focus for the interview should also be positive, encouraging the person to come up with some helpful improvements and inferring that their input is valued. (Of course this should have happened while the individual was still on the staff, but too late now!) The interview also offers the opportunity for closure. Psychologically, people need to feel that something has finished well, and the time taken for a formal farewell is generally appreciated. Just as it is important to never send an unhappy customer away, it is important to never send an unhappy staff member away.

Thus, the benefits of conducting an exit interview are:

- it allows for a formal closure to the employee's term of service;
- it enables the employer to explore a number of job satisfaction issues in detail;
- it enables the employer to explore ideas for change in service provision;
- it enables departing employees to feel valued;

EXIT INTERVIEW FORMAT

Thank the person for making the time to be interviewed.

Explore reasons for leaving and plans for the future.

Ask for suggestions for improvements in, for example,

> job expectations
> job satisfaction
> customer satisfaction
> procedures
> products
> working environment
> relationships with colleagues
> supervision
> training and career development.

Ask the person about their views on possible changes to consumer behaviour in the future, and the impact they see this having on your operation.

Ensure that the person has returned keys, ID's etc.

Wish the person well in the future and farewell.

- it gives the employer an opportunity to resolve outstanding issues, if any;
- it provides a good opportunity to check that necessary items have been returned;
- outstanding paperwork can be completed and handed over, such as statement of service and tax certificates;
- it enables the employer to farewell the employee and wish them success in the future.

TURNOVER RATE

Most large organisations calculate the rate of employee turnover using the following formula:

$$\frac{\text{number of staff leaving per annum}}{\text{total number of staff}} \times 100$$

This figure is not, however, as meaningful as one would hope. If there was 100 per cent turnover, would that mean a customer who had not visited the store for a year would recognise none of the staff? This is unlikely. There are generally some positions that have a high turnover and some that have a low turnover. Supervisory and management staff tend to stay longer, and it would be a sorry day indeed if high turnover were experienced in senior ranks. Many service organisations have

EXIT INTERVIEW REPORT FORM

Reasons for leaving?

_____

_____

Alternative employment?

_____

_____

Comments relating to job satisfaction?

_____

_____

How would you describe employee morale?

_____

_____

How would you describe working conditions?

_____

_____

How would you describe relationships between staff in the department?

_____

_____

How would you describe the management of the department?

_____

_____

What were your expectations of the job when you started?

_____

_____

Do you think the company was able to meet your career aspirations?

_____

_____

Which of our customers do you think are the most important?

_____

_____

Do you have any suggestions for better meeting the needs of these customers?

_____

_____

Are there any general suggestions you have?

_____

_____

_____

_____

Conclude paperwork, keys or uniforms and any outstanding procedures completed.

List of items handed to employee

Severance pay	[ ]	*Other*
Statement of service	[ ]	_____
Taxation certificate	[ ]	_____

[Signed]
Manager

turnover rates over 200 per cent! This means that some jobs are changing several times during the year, and that the average employee in these positions stays for only a few months. Hopefully you managers of the future will not see staff in these important roles as being expendable: previous chapters have illustrated the high-level skills required for customer service.

Most organisations calculate the turnover rate by department, by shift or by position in order to pick up trends. This is useful only where there are large numbers of employees. If one person out of three leaves, this is calculated as a 30 per cent annual turnover rate.

Stability index

Another useful index is the stability index. This measures the percentage of staff who have been with the organisation for over twelve months. In a small department, a large percentage of long service staff may leave, the remaining staff also having been with the organisation for many years; the stability index could show this, and contrast this department with another, where little turnover has been experienced but stability is low. The turnover percentage and the stability index can be used as two different measures for analysis of staff changes.

$$\frac{\text{number of staff with 12 months' service}}{\text{total number of staff}} \times 100$$

Usually these percentages are calculated for full-time staff only, as they can be extremely deceptive where a large number of casual staff are employed. Investment in human resources cannot take place if a large number of casual staff are employed. Organisations should look towards more flexible working hours as part of the employment contract in order to solve this problem. This would achieve a cost saving and at the same time allow for the development of a committed, cohesive and stable work force.

THE COST OF EMPLOYMENT

The cost of recruitment, selection and training for a new member of staff is far higher than one would expect. It is possible to calculate the costs for a position in the service industry. Where time is a factor this should be costed out with an estimate of the time taken and the person's hourly rate. These roles could vary— some being secretarial, others the manager or Personnel Officer.

Recruitment and selection costs

Advertising—internal
Lead time cost (where positions are widely advertised with extended application periods, it can take months to fill a position, and there is a productivity cost for the unfilled position)
Time spent preparing advertisement (including desk-top publishing)

Advertising—external (for example, newspapers)
Time taken to answer calls
Time taken to review resumes
Time taken to respond to unsuccessful applicants
Stationery and postage
Verification of applicant details, reference checking
Time taken to narrow down short list
Time taken to interview applicants
Time taken to respond to unsuccessful short-list applicants
Time taken to respond to enquiries about progress
Time taken for second interviews
Time taken to write letter of appointment
Time taken to write to unsuccessful final candidates
Testing (such as work samples)
Medical.

Induction and training costs

From the moment the new employee starts, there are two costs for time and pay: for the new employee *and* the person who is doing the induction or training. It is necessary to estimate how long it is going to take before the employee is 100 per cent productive. Anything less than this level of productivity is a further cost.

Time taken for employment record keeping and processing of documentation
Time taken for induction (employee *and* supervisor)
Preparation of induction materials
Cost of employee handbook
Cost of formal orientation session (divided by the number of participants)
Time taken for training (employee *and* supervisor/other staff)—this can be worked out over a period of time with a number of hours per day, or a percentage of time allocated to training
Time taken by payroll department with data entry, deductions, direct banking and so on
Taxes, such as payroll and premiums for Worker's Compensation insurance
Uniforms.

In Figure 14.1, a new employee has taken two weeks to reach full productivity. Lost productivity is clearly very high in the first week, diminishing in the second week. In more senior positions, reaching full productivity could take longer and thus the learning curve could be a different shape, depending on the complexity of the job.

Separation costs

Time taken for counselling (both employee *and* supervisor)
Time taken for disciplinary procedure implementation (for example, letters)
Possible legal advice

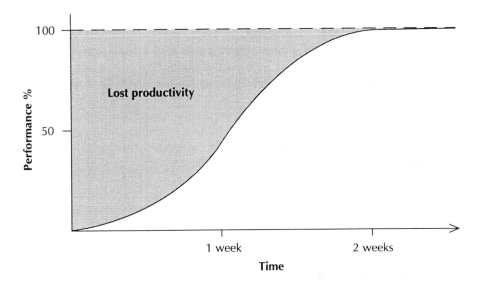

Figure 14.1   Time taken for new employee to achieve 100 per cent productivity

Severance pay
Cost of exit interview
Time taken for termination record keeping and processing
Possible legal costs arising as a result of termination.

Indirect costs

In addition to the direct costs arising from poor selection decisions, there are indirect costs. These include the cost of accidents, poor morale, low productivity and the effect of poor service on revenue. One can estimate the following costs for an employee who does not meet performance standards:

Minor damage to merchandise, equipment, breakages
Cost of accidents
Cost of lost custom resulting from the low productivity of all staff where morale is affected
Cost of lost custom when a dissatisfied customer leaves and talks about the poor service to a number of other potential customers
Cost of overtime while a substitute employee is recruited and selected.

Overall costs based on labour turnover

Having made a rough calculation of the costs for the employment and departure of one employee, this figure is then multiplied by the average number of employees leaving in a year. This will give an estimate of direct cost of staff turnover.

In addition to the direct costs of labour turnover (that is, the cost of replacing staff who leave), there are indirect costs which are harder to quantify. They include such things as costs relating to customer dissatisfaction and defection to competitors, costs relating to inefficiency and costs relating to lost business caused by inadequately trained staff while the organisation struggles to keep up with the need for competent personnel.

Ten per cent of actual revenue is a good estimate for the indirect cost of high labour turnover. However difficult it may be to estimate these indirect costs, estimates are valuable in demonstrating the importance of retaining good staff.

EXERCISES AND DISCUSSION

1. Use the suggested exit interview format or your own improved version to interview someone about their last job.

2. Using the results of your exit interview, evaluate such interviews as a technique for obtaining valuable feedback.

3. From the individual's point of view, what value does an interview have for them when they are leaving?

|15

ETHICS IN SERVICE

SUMMARY

This chapter raises some important ethical questions in relation to service. In some situations service should be refused, but mangers rather turn a blind eye rather than watch profits walk out the door. In many businesses, human resource management is compromised by budgetary restraint. How much can a business really afford to invest in its people? These questions and many more will be raised in this chapter.

CHAPTER OBJECTIVES

On completion of this chapter you will be able to:

- discuss several contemporary issues from an ethical standpoint;
- develop a code of service ethics;
- apply concepts covered in the text to a case studies with ethical considerations;
- explain the concept of employee empowerment.

ETHICS IN SERVICE

Labour costs are high in the service industry, and efforts to reduce this cost include the employment of large numbers of casual employees, wage payments in cash, accommodation and meals in lieu of payment, and many other such arrangements. Even in organisations whose conduct is legally above board, there is the ethical consideration of how much service to provide, balanced against the need to make a profit. Let's face it: quality service comes at a price. With adequate numbers of trained staff on duty, anyone can provide good service. The reality of life is that managers are under pressure to control costs, and the use of a large casual work force can keep these costs under control in the short-term. There is a fine line between providing quality service and making a profit. This is the ethical dilemma faced by managers in service industries each and every day, even though most are not conscious of it.

It has been argued in this book that sound human resources planning and management, although coming at a cost, is the only way to reach long-term, sustainable profits, by providing quality service. Provision of quality service will increase profits by establishing a good client base and reputation. Management has a commitment to the community in the provision of services advertised, and it has a commitment to its employees to provide secure employment, skill development and a workplace in which they are not subjected to undue pressure.

Stress levels are high in the services sector, employees suffering from burn out as a result of shift work and undue pressures during busy periods when customers' demands cannot be met. Many accept it as the nature of the industry. Management, however, seems to escape the blame for understaffing, poor rostering, shortages of supplies, faulty equipment and other similar hurdles that prevent front-line staff from providing good service. In most cases, these problems stem from a lack of planning, but in many others they stem from a desire to make the bottom line look good; cutting costs is a sure way to achieve this in the short-term. Unfortunately for the employee that faces the customer, the blame for poor service is nearly always attributed to them, and staff are then expected to carry this emotional burden. This is not often recognised, and employees handling complaints are never supposed to make excuses or lay blame. They are expected to take it on the chin, 'cop it sweet' and resolve the situation to the customer's satisfaction. Imagine a staff member saying to a customer, 'Sorry mate, the manager is trying to reduce costs, and she has left us understaffed today. Just not enough trained staff to go around. You'll have to wait.'

EMPLOYEE EMPOWERMENT

An emerging concept is that of employee empowerment. Empowerment gives employees greater responsibility for resolving issues for customers. Staff at Ritz Carlton hotels are able to exercise their own discretion in solving guest complaints up to a pre-set limit without involving more senior staff. This enables them to immediately implement solutions and widens their responsibility and authority.

Empowerment alone is not satisfactory. It needs to be backed up by sound management practices that prevent the occurrence of incidents leading to complaints. This entails careful planning, implementation of policies and procedures and continuous evaluation. The focus for this effort by management should be ensuring quality assurance, with cost control only secondary to this aim. This may seem a small shift in thinking, but in reality it is not by any means. Management thinking in the past has been negatively oriented, as cost control is a negative concept. It implies that money is wasted, trimming is necessary and the wages budget, being the largest, is the best starting point. Quality assurance, on the other hand, looks at ways in which management efforts can be directed towards long-term, sustainable profit based on customer satisfaction.

WILL IT COME to this? If Sydney has water restrictions, will they be as severe as Peter Johnson, of Killara, found in Phoenix, Arizona, three years ago? He has two cards, souvenired from restaurants. They say the same sort of thing: "To help us conserve this environment, water will be served only upon request. Please ask your waiter/waitress for a glass." And this in the country where a glass of iced water is at every table setting.
(*SMH*, 5/10/94)

From the employees' viewpoint, this should mean secure, permanent employment, training and development, and empowerment to ensure the satisfaction guaranteed to customers.

Kapoor and Kapoor (1992) cite the example of Marriot Hotels, whose aim is to empower staff to meet customer service guarantees. According to its Human Resources Manager, 'The foundation of empowerment is the belief that outstanding service requires front-line employees who are trained, equipped, authorized and trusted to meet or exceed customer expectations and needs' (Kapoor & Kapoor 1992, p. 46). They illustrate this point by describing an incident with a guest:

The room service operator received a call from a very distraught guest. The guest wanted to cancel an order she had placed a few minutes earlier. Noticing her distress, the operator asked the guest if she was OK. The guest told the operator she had just received a call from her brother. Her mother in California had suffered a massive stroke and was not expected to survive the night. She had called the airlines to schedule a flight. They told her that there was only one flight out and it was leaving in 35 minutes. Realizing that she could not make it to the airport in time, she made a reservation for the next morning. She was cancelling her room service order because she was too upset to eat.

The room service operator jumped into action. She called the restaurant hostess, briefly informed her of the problem and forwarded the room service phones to the restaurant. She hurried to the guest's room, greeted her with a hug, told her to quickly pack and that she would take her to the airport. While the guest was packing she called the airline, changed the flight reservation, called the front desk to prepare the guest's bill and the bell desk to get her bags.

Because of the operator's actions, the guest was able to arrive at her mother's bedside before she passed away that night.

(Kapoor & Kapoor 1992, p. 47)

DEVELOPING A CODE OF ETHICS

In developing a company code of ethics, there are some of the aspects that could be reviewed in relation to service:

- Look at advertising ethics and ask 'How accurately is our product or service portrayed?'
- Look at external customer service ethics and ask 'How will we ensure that we meet customer expectations?'
- Look at internal customer service ethics and ask 'How will we ensure co-operation between departments and individuals?'
- Look at human resource management ethics and ask 'How will we ensure adequate staffing, training and career development, security of employment, and employee participation?'

Hall (1992)* suggests the following tests for deciding what ought to be done when making decisions and developing a company code of ethics.

Is the decision legal?

In many small businesses, staff are paid cash, tax is not deducted and workers are not insured. Illegal migrants are employed at rates far below the minimum wage, are paid in cash and told that they cannot expect the normal legal entitlements due to them such as overtime.

Extended periods of 'trial' are often used to utilise cost-free labour for menial tasks. One such case illustrates the point. A new receptionist was employed by a small motel, trained on Friday and asked to take care of things over the weekend. She was nervous but coped reasonably well, handling check-ins, payments etc. The following week when she asked about payment she was told that she had been on 'trial' for the first three days.

Is the decision fair?

Reducing labour cost by increasing the number of casual employees places extra burdens on permanent staff. Employing staff of only a certain age or appearance is not only illegal but also unfair. One applicant, when she asked why she hadn't been successful in getting the job, was told by the manager to look around her. She did and asked, 'What are you talking about?' His response was 'I only employ blondes under five foot five'.

Does the decision hurt anyone?

Although lip service is paid to promotion from within, this policy is seldom adhered to in any reasonable sense. It would appear that for employers, the grass is always

* Reprinted with permission from *Ethics in Hospitality Management* by S. J. Hall. Copyright by the Educational Institute of the American Hotel & Motel Association, PO Box 1240, East Lansing, Mich., 48836–1240. All rights reserved.

greener. The people out there must be better than the bunch we have here. All too often staff newly employed for management and supervisory positions are not as well qualified or as experienced as some of the current employees. This results in tremendous frustration, especially when talented individuals are typecast into roles having 'started at the bottom' as advised when they began with the organisation. Within a short period their qualifications are forgotten and their career prospects diminished.

Have I been honest with those affected?

Anxiety can build up very quickly when staff sense that the organisation is not doing well. Management often shares its decisions only when they are positive ones, failing to reassure or inform where hard decisions have to be taken. If staff cuts are necessary, these decisions should be made quickly and implemented immediately. Speculation about this or any other issue is harmful to morale. Management honesty is appreciated and builds loyalty.

Can I live with my decision?

Finally, there is the inner sense of what is right, and this should lead to the acceptance that the decision was appropriate. The decision to refuse to serve alcohol to someone who has clearly had too much is one of the most difficult to make in the service industry. This is a very fine line, since the evaluation of what is 'too much' would vary from individual. In the worst case, a non-drinker would send everyone home after a few drinks and the place would be deserted after a few days. Many customers visit bars with the purpose of drinking for relaxation and bars make a profit by selling as much alcohol as possible. The ethical dilemma has been raised in the industry where special promotions, dollar drinks and the like ensure that young people are overexposed to the dangers of alcohol. This is particularly the case with 'happy hours' where patrons are encouraged by drink prices to consume as much as possible in the shortest possible time.

The stages involved in building a code of ethics are as follows:

- Discussions with staff and customers—Discuss in focus groups some of the ethical issues that face your type of operation.

- Development of a code of ethics—Management and staff should work towards developing a code of ethics such as the example given here.

- Communicate and implement the code of ethics—Staff should be aware of the code of ethics, and it should form part of the employee handbook. They should be reminded of its contents from time to time, and discussions relating to issues should occur in staff meetings.

Tellers have different tale on their bank's $5 offer

An offer by the ANZ Bank to pay its customers $5 every time they wait more than five minutes for service has hit a snag—the bank tellers' union is dead against it.

The assistant national secretary of the Finance Sector Union, Mr Barry Hirt, said yesterday that the union commended any initiative aimed at improving service to bank customers.

But ANZ's $5 offer was a "quick-fix marketing tool" which could increase the stress levels of bank tellers, Mr Hirt said.

A reduction in customer service could result from tellers rushing to complete transactions within five minutes at the expense of meeting individual needs.

ANZ has introduced the $5 teller queue guarantee, also known as "strive for five", as part of a major staff reshuffle.

In future, all ANZ staff in metropolitan branches will serve customers. None will undertake telephone or paperwork at desks behind counters.

Extra part-time tellers will be rostered on during peak customer times such as lunch hours to meet the service deadline.

An ANZ spokesman, Mr David Brown, said that a survey of the bank's customers had found a major complaint was the waiting time in queues.

ANZ had remedied the problem by assigning project teams with stopwatches to bank branches and then adjusting staff numbers to speed up service, Mr Brown said.

Each branch of the bank now guaranteed to serve 90 per cent of customers within three minutes of their joining a queue and 99 per cent within five minutes.

If not served within five minutes, a customer could give the teller his or her name, address and account number. The teller then initialled a bank slip with the customer's details and $5 would be credited to the relevant account overnight.

Mr Brown described as unfortunate opposition from the Finance Sector Union, which he said had been briefed about the scheme and had supported the idea at the time.

Fears that tellers would be put under too much pressure were unfounded, he said. The scheme had been tested for 18 months and the bank knew that staff could deliver the five-minute standard.

"There will be no pressure on staff to make sure they don't hand out too many $5. The fact is that staff are not being asked to do anything they haven't done for 18 months. It's a vote of confidence in our staff."

The concept of free offers or benefits for customers who experience slow service has been used in the past by fast food chains such as McDonald's. But this is the first time a bank has opted for cash payment for slow service.

Mr Brown said: "Some people may say $5 is not a lot of money, but we're putting our money where our mouth is".

—Brad Norington
(*SMH*, 16/6/94)

REVIEW AND EVALUATION

Changes to the organisation and its operation may change the code of ethics. Problems and incidents often raise the sorts of issues that form part of ethical considerations. Requests by customers for alcohol service when under-age, assistance in the purchase of illegal drugs or harassment perpetrated by customers on staff are some examples of issues that may require discussion. From another point of view, discrepancies in the till, pilferage and other staff actions may need to be discussed. Where the conduct of the organisation is not ethical, for example, cheap alcohol is substituted for higher-priced drinks, employee conduct will follow the example of management.

EXAMPLE CODE OF SERVICE ETHICS

Each business decision will be tested against standards of honesty, integrity and fair dealing.

We will conduct our activities in an ethical manner, in so far as they concern our staff, our customers and our suppliers.

We will treat all customers and employees equally.

We will provide consistency across all procedures.

We will provide a high standard of care for customers and staff, ensuring their health and safety.

We will provide every employee with clear guidelines, with training and support in their efforts to achieve customer satisfaction.

Employees will have equal rights to progression in their employment based on merit.

EXERCISES AND DISCUSSION

1. Discuss the following contemporary issues from an ethical viewpoint:

> High rates of casual employment
> High staff turnover
> Cash payments for wages
> Staff drinking while on duty or at lunch
> Turning a blind eye to pilferage
> Excessive pricing
> Hidden costs, not immediately disclosed to customers
> High stress levels
> Job security
> Discrimination
> Exposure of staff to health risks
> Overbooking.

2. As the owner of a small business you are faced with recession. As a result, you need to reduce your staff costs, possibly by making one of your least effective salespeople redundant and employing a casual to take his place during busy periods. You have a very cohesive group of employees who have been with you for a long time. They aren't going to like this, and morale is going to slump. How should you approach this?

3. As the bar manager of a small pub, you are faced with the problem of harassment of staff by patrons. They want to know how much they are expected to tolerate. How would you approach this?

4. You have a casual employee who has been working for you in the purchasing department for over eighteen months. She has always been an outstanding employee giving excellent value because of her expertise and hard work. Six months ago her husband left her and she has had to sell the house and resolve all her financial affairs. This has entailed numerous phone calls during working hours, and occasionally some time off. She has also been quite distraught about the whole thing, but other staff have taken her under their wing. Now it appears that she has a health problem and although not entitled to sick leave, will not be able to work as required for the next few months. She is only a casual, and could be replaced without any difficulty. If you keep her on, her attendance will be sporadic for the next few months at least, and you will have to employ another casual to fill the gaps. Should you replace her?

5. If you owned a small business, what would you call a 'fair' profit after paying yourself a 'reasonable' wage?

GLOSSARY

ACTIVE LISTENING is a technique in which the listener pays attention to the whole message, that is, the content and the feeling.

APPRAISAL refers to evaluation against expectations or the ideal performance.

ARTEFACTS are objects used to convey non-verbal messages about image, style and ambience.

ASSESSMENT is the process of forming a judgement about a performance or product against performance criteria in a statement of standards. *

ATTRIBUTE is a characteristic quality recognised as appropriate.

BENCHMARKING is a method for continuous systematic comparison of the products, services and processes of an organisation with the best practices, both locally and globally.

COMMUNICATION is any behaviour, verbal or non-verbal, that is perceived by another.

COMPETENCY is the ability to perform the activities within an occupation or function to the standard expected in employment. *

COMPETENCY BASED TRAINING (CBT) is training concerned with the attainment and demonstration of specified skills, knowledge and their application to meet industry standards rather than with an individual's achievement relative to a group. *

COMPETENCY LEVEL is part of an agreed framework against which vocational training and qualifications many be compared. *

CLOSED QUESTION is a question designed to limit the response to a 'yes' or 'no' answer.

---

* National Training Board definition, reproduced with permission.

CRITERION-REFERENCED ASSESSMENT refers to the collection of evidence about a person's performance and judging the nature and extent of progress towards the requirements specified in clearly defined performance criteria or assessment criteria.

CRITICAL INCIDENT TECHNIQUE is a one-to-one interview carried out by a person skilled in the technique which requires participants to focus on significant work incidents from their past and the competencies which enabled them to perform successfully. The technique focuses on the underlying attributes and individual characteristics of successful performance rather than on routine duties. *

EMPOWERMENT is where employees are more autonomous, responsible for their own work, and can make decisions relating to their work.

EXIT INTERVIEW is an interview held for staff leaving the organisation. It provides the opportunity to obtain feedback and suggestions, to resolve final issues and to wish the departing employee success in the future.

FEEDBACK is the receiver's response to a sender's message which tells the sender how their message is being received and helps the receiver confirm whether their perception of the message is correct.

FRONT-LINE STAFF are staff that have direct contact with customers, by means of face-to-face communication, telephone, letter, fax or any other channel.

FUNCTIONAL JOB ANALYSIS is an information collection technique using group participation, usually by the lead bodies or representative peak training organisation in an industry, and a skilled facilitator to establish the competency standards for an occupation. It identifies:

- the key purpose or function of the occupation in terms of outcome;
- the elements of competency which allow the key purpose to be achieved;
- the performance criteria for each task identified as necessary for competency.*

HOLISTIC ASSESSMENT refers to an approach to competency-based assessment that covers, in an integrated way, multiple elements and/or units from relevant competency standards. The integrated approach seeks to combine knowledge, understanding, problem-solving, technical skills attitudes and ethics into assessment tasks. (Hagar, Athanasou & Gonczi 1994)

JOB ANALYSIS is the system of breaking a job down into various elements— including the description of duties, the skill and experience requirements—for various purposes.

JOB DESCRIPTION describes the position, lines of communication, duties and conditions of employment.

JOB ENRICHMENT is the attempt to improve a job by adding motivational factors such as responsibility, decision-making, variety and challenge.

JOB SPECIFICATION (or person specification) describes the ideal applicant for the job in terms of skill, experience and other attributes.

MESSAGE is the idea or feeling transmitted from the sender to the receiver to achieve understanding.

MODELLING is where trainees copy role models in the imitation of behaviour.

MOTIVATION is the inner force that drives behaviour.

MULTISKILLING is the ability to perform a wide range of tasks.

NON-VERBAL COMMUNICATION is communication that is sent by any means other than words.

OPEN QUESTION is a question phrased in such a way that it elicits a lengthy response.

RECOGNITION OF PRIOR LEARNING (RPL) refers to determination on an individual basis of the competencies obtained by a person through previous formal or in-formal training, work experience and/or life experience. *

RELIABILITY refers to the extent in which consistent outcomes are achieved in assessment.

SKILL may be perceptual, motor, manual, intellectual, social. The nature of tasks usually requires a combination of these and usually involves the application of cognitive and psychomotor functions, together with appropriate knowledge. *

STABILITY INDEX is calculated by the number of staff who have been employed for over one year divided by the total number of staff, expressed as a percentage.

STAFF TURNOVER is calculated by the number of staff who have left divided by the total number of employees.

STANDARD is a statement in outcome terms of what is expected of an individual performing a particular occupational role. *

TASK is a discrete, identifiable and meaningful unit of work that is carried out by the job-holder for a specific purpose leading to a specific outcome. The performance of a task requires the application of skill. *

TOTAL QUALITY MANAGEMENT involves a commitment to quality, the development of quality systems and the measurement of quality improvement.

TRAINING OBJECTIVE is a clear statement of what learners should be able to do, the conditions under which this performance occurs, and the criteria by which successful performance is measured.

VALIDITY refers to the extent to which the assessment measures what it claims to measure.

BIBLIOGRAPHY

Australian Education Council Review Committee 1991, *Young People's Participation in Post-Compulsory Education and Training* (B. Finn, Chairman), AGPS, Canberra.

Australian Standards 1991, *Quality Management and Quality System Elements, Part 2: Guidelines for Services (AS 3904.2–1992, NZS 9004.2:1992, ISO 9004-2:1991)*, Standards Australia, Sydney (and Standards Association of New Zealand, Wellington).

Bandura, A. & Walters, R. 1977, *Social Learning Theory*, Prentice-Hall, Englewood Cliffs, NJ.

Bloom, B. S., Englehart, M. D., Furst, E. J., Hill, W. H. & Krathwohl, D. R. 1956, *Taxonomy of Educational Objectives, Handbook 1: The Cognitive Domain*, David McKay, New York.

Bolton, R. 1987, *People Skills: How to Assert Yourself, Listen to Others and Resolve Conflicts*, Simon & Schuster, Sydney.

Bolton, R. 1991 (1987), *People Skills: How to Assert Yourself, Listen to Others and Resolve Conflicts*, Simon & Schuster, Sydney.

Boud, D. (ed.) 1985, *Reflection: Turning Experience into Learning*, Kogan Page, London.

Boud, D. (ed.) 1988, *Developing Student Autonomy in Learning*, Kogan Page, London.

Burg, F. D., Lloyd, J. S. & Templeton, B. 1982, Competence in Medicine, *Medical Teacher*, vol. 4, no. 2.

Burns, R. 1993, *Managing People in Changing Times*, Allen & Unwin, Sydney.

Candy, P. 1988, 'On the Attainment of Subject-matter Autonomy', in *Developing Student Autonomy in Learning*, ed. D. Boud, Kogan Page, London.

Carlzon, J. 1987, *Moments of Truth*, Harper & Rowe, New York.

Clarke, R. 1988, *Australian Human Resources Management*, McGraw-Hill, Sydney.

Commonwealth State Training Advisory Committee (COSTAC) Working Party 1990, *A Strategic Framework for the Implementation of a Competency Based Training System*, AGPS, Canberra.

Compton, R. & Nankervis, A. 1991, *Effective Selection and Recruitment Practices*, CCH Personnel Management in Practice Series, CCH Australia, Sydney.

Cooper, L. O. 1991, Toward a theory of listening competency: the development of a two-factor model of listening in organizations, PhD thesis, University of Illinois at Urbana-Champaign.

Day, M. 1994, *Daily Telegraph Mirror*, 5 July, p. 10.

Delia, J. G., O'Keefe, B. J. & O'Keefe, D. J. 1982, The constructivist approach to communication, in *Human Communication Theory: Comparative Essays*, ed. F. Dance, Harper & Rowe, New York.

Delia, J. G. & Swanson, D. L. 1976, *The Nature of Human Communication, Modcom Modules in Speech Communication*, Science Research Associates, Chicago, Ill.

Dwyer, J. 1993, *The Business Communication Handbook*, Prentice-Hall, Sydney.

Egan, G. 1988a, *Change Agent Skills A: Assessing and Designing Excellence*, Pfeiffer, San Diego, Calif.

Egan, G. 1988b, *Change Agent Skills B: Managing Innovation and Change*, Pfeiffer, San Diego, Calif.

Eunson, B. 1987, *Behaving, Managing Yourself and Others*, McGraw-Hill, Sydney.

Evans, G. & Butler, J. 1992, Thinking and enhanced performance in the workplace, Paper presented at 5th International Conference on Thinking, Townsville, Qld.

Field, L. 1990, *Skilling Australia*, Longman Cheshire, Sydney.

Finn Report. See Australian Education Council Review Committee.

Fletcher, S. 1993, *Quality and Competence: Integrating Competence and Quality Initiatives*, Kogan Page, London.

Fox, R. 1991, *Making Quality Happen: Six Steps to Total Quality Management*, McGraw-Hill, Sydney.

Gerson, R. 1992, *Beyond Customer Service: Keeping Customers for Life*, Crisp Publications, Menlo Park, Calif.

Gonczi, A. (ed.) 1992, *Developing a Competent Workforce*, National Centre for Vocational Education Research, Canberra.

Gonczi, A., Hager, P. & Athanasou, J. 1993, The Development of Competency-based Assessment Strategies for the Professions, NOOSR Research Paper 8, AGPS, Canberra.

Gonczi A., Hager, P. & Oliver, L. 1990, Competency approaches to education, Paper presented at the Annual Conference of the Australian Association for Research in Education, University of Sydney, Nov.

Gonczi, A., Palmer, C. & Hager, P. 1994, Competency based assessment—The NSW Law Society specialist accreditation program, Paper presented at the 1994 Professional Legal Skills Conference, Bond University, Gold Coast, Qld.

Green, P. C. 1982, *Behavioural Interviewing*, Industrial Organizational Psychologists, Memphis, Tenn.

Griffiths D. N. 1990, *Implementing Quality with a Customer Focus*, ASQC Quality Press, Milwaukee, Wis.

Hager, P., Athanasou, J. & Gonczi, A. 1994, *Assessment Technical Manual*, Department of Education, Employment and Training, Canberra, in assoc. with AGPS, Canberra.

Hall, S. J. (ed.) 1992, *Ethics in Hospitality Management: A Book of Readings*, Educational Institute of the American Hotel & Motel Association, East Lansing, Mich.

Hall, W. & Saunders, J. 1994, *Getting to Grips with Assessment*, National Centre for Vocational Education Research, SA.

Heron, J. 1988, Assessment revisited, in *Developing Student Autonomy in Learning*, ed. D. Boud, Kogan Page, London.

Heron, J. 1989, *The Facilitator's Handbook*, Kogan Page, London.

Higgs, J. 1988, Planning learning experiences to promote autonomous learning, in *Developing Student Autonomy in Learning*, ed. D. Boud, Kogan Page, London.

Holt, M. (ed.) 1987, *Skills and Vocationalism: The Easy Answer*, Open University Press, Milton Keynes.

Kapoor, T. & Kapoor, S. 1992, Ethically empowering others to win, in *Ethics in Hospitality Management: A Book of Readings*, ed. S. J. Hall, Educational Institute of the American Hotel & Motel Association, East Lansing, Mich.

Kaye, M. 1992, Adult communication management in adult vocational education: a contemporary Australian perspective, Paper presented to 42nd Annual Conference International Communication Association, Miami, Fla., 21–25 May.

Kaye, M. & McArthur, S. 1989, The criterion of 'good communication skills' in job advertisements, Paper presented to Annual Conference of Australian Communication Association, Queensland University of Technology, Brisbane, 13–15 July.

Knowles, M. 1973, *The Adult Learner: A Neglected Species*, Gulf Publishing, London.

Knowles, M. 1984, *The Adult Learner: A Neglected Species*, 3rd edn, Gulf Publishing, Houston, Tex.

Kolb, D. 1984, *Experiential Learning*, Prentice-Hall, Englewood Cliffs, NJ.

Lindeman, E. C. 1926, *The Meaning of Adult Education*, New Republic, New York.

Mackay, H. 1993, *Reinventing Australia: The Mind and Mood of Australia in the 90's*, Angus & Robertson, Sydney.

Martin, W. B. 1989, *Managing Quality Customer Service*, Crisp Publications, Los Altos, Calif.

Martin, W. B. 1993, *Quality Customer Service*, 3rd edn, Crisp Publications, Los Altos, Calif.

Mayer Committee 1992, Employment-related Key Competencies for Post-compulsory Education and Training: A Discussion Paper (E. Mayer, Chairman), AGPS, Canberra.

Middlebrook, P. 1980, *Social Psychology and Modern Life*, Alfred A. Knopf, New York.

National Centre for Competency Based Training 1993, *Implementing CBT*, AGPS, Canberra.

National Training Board (NTB) 1992, *Policy and Guidelines*, 2nd edn, NTB, Canberra.

Norington, B. 1994, 'Tellers have a different tale on their bank's $5 offer', *Sydney Morning Herald*, 16 June, p. 3

O'Keefe, D. J. 1990, *Persuasion, Theory and Research*, Sage Publications, London.

Peters, T. J. & Waterman, R. H. 1982, *In Search of Excellence: Lessons from America's Best-run Companies*, Harper & Rowe, New York.

Reilly, N. B. 1994, *Quality: What Makes it Happen?*, Van Nostrand Reinhold, New York.

Robbins, S., Low, P. & Mourell, M. 1986, *Managing Human Resources*, Prentice-Hall, Sydney.

Schuleer, R., Dowling, P., Smart, J. & Huber, S. 1992, *Human Resource Management in Australia*, 2nd edn, Harper International, Sydney.

'Service expectations across hospitality sectors, local and international visitors' 1994, Unpublished research by students of the Associate Diploma of Tourism and Hospitality, Northern Beaches College of TAFE, Brookvale, Sydney.

Splitter, L. 1991, 'Critical thinking: what, why, when and how', *Educational Philosophy and Theory*, vol. 23, no. 1, pp. 81–109.

Sydney Morning Herald 1994, 'Column 8' (p. 1) 12 June, 13 June, 22 June, 23 June, 25 June, 1 July, 19 July, 23 July, 26 July, 11 Aug., 6 Sept., 22 Sept., 3 Oct., 5 Oct., 8 Oct.,

Thomas, A. M. 1991, *Beyond Education: A New Perspective on Society's Management of Learning*, Jossey-Bass, San Francisco, Calif.

Toop, L., Gibb, J. & Worsnop, P. 1994, *Assessment System Design*, AGPS, Canberra.

Tylczak, L. 1990, *Increasing Employee Productivity: An Introduction to Value Management*, Crisp Publications, Los Antos, Calif.

Urquhart, B. 1991, *Serves You Right*, Marketing Focus, Kalamuda, WA.

VEETAC Working Party on the Implementation of Competency-based Training, 1992, *Assessment of Performance under Competency-based Training*, AGPS, Canberra.

Vogt, J. & Murrel, K. 1990, *Empowerment in Organisations: How to Spark Exceptional Performance*, Pfeiffer, San Diego Calif.

Vroom, V. 1964, *Work and Motivation*, Wiley, New York.

Wheelhouse, D. 1989, *Managing Human Resources in the Hospitality Industry*, Educational Institute of the American Hotel & Motel Association, East Lansing, Mich.

Wolf, A. 1993, Assessment issues and problems in a criterion-based system, A Further Education Unit Occasional Paper, Sydney.

Zeithamel, V., Parasuraman, A. & Berry, L. 1990, *Delivering Quality Service: Balancing Customer Perceptions and Expectations*, Free Press, New York.

INDEX

NOTES